The Old Mill Creek

The Old Mill Creek

The Park Collection

JAMES E. McCOLLUM

RESOURCE *Publications* · Eugene, Oregon

THE OLD MILL CREEK
The Park Collection

Resource Publications
An Imprint of Wipf and Stock Publishers
199 W. 8th Ave., Suite 3
Eugene, OR 97401

www.wipfandstock.com

PAPERBACK ISBN: 978-1-7252-7821-9
HARDCOVER ISBN: 978-1-7252-7822-6
EBOOK ISBN: 978-1-7252-7823-3

Manufactured in the U.S.A.   10/12/20

This one is for Annemarie and Eric, with abiding love and pride. The world is a better place because of each of you.

Contents

Preface | ix
Acknowledgements | xiii

Star-Crossed Lovers, Nevermore | 1
The Rose | 23
A Compass Pointing West | 25
The Old Home Cemetery | 43
The Caretaker | 46
Magic in the Trees | 50
The Dragon's Lair | 57
The Miracle within the Polished Stone | 75

Photos | 91

Preface

I GREW UP IN Youngstown, Ohio. My father's ancestors, the McCollum's and the Kyle's, were among the earliest settlers in Austintown, Canfield, and Youngstown. My father and his siblings were the last McCollum's born, and who lived in the historic Kyle-McCollum homestead built by Joshua and Mary Stewart Kyle, begun in 1798 and completed around 1812. The Kyle's daughter, Hannah, married Ira McCollum, the son of the first settlers of Austintown, John and Jayne Ayers McCollum. From that time on, until my father was a teenager in the 1930s, the homestead was a McCollum residence. The historic homestead, adjacent to Mill Creek Park, nestled quietly at the end of McCollum Road and diagonal from the Home Cemetery, is today the oldest continuously occupied residence in Youngstown. As a child, I lived close by, off Belle Vista Road, and roamed the park as if it were my private estate and preserve. The love and appreciation I have for the wonderous miracles of nature were nurtured into my soul from my early experience of the crown jewel of Youngstown, Ohio; the natural wonder my father reverently called the *Old Mill Creek.*

Each poem within this collection, whether historically based, fictional, or fantasy has some connection with or to my father's sacred ground, the *Old Mill Creek.* The Park Collection, as I have subtitled it, is a work of love; love of family, love of nature, and love of the confounding mystery of life. The poems I offer to you to read and enjoy, despite the common element of the park, are diverse. A quick account of what to expect follows.

Star-crossed Lovers Nevermore is a poem inspired by Shakespeare's *Romeo and Juliet,* a fantasy of a dragon overlord, an eagle, two love-torn sparrows, and other birds whose lives were recorded in the *Chronicles of Avian*. A drawing of a beautiful red rose free from its tangled background, drawn by my granddaughter, Claire, was the animus, my muse, for *The Rose*. I found disquieting inspiration within our country's history of immigration and migration, and the current controversies swirling around who should be welcomed to settle in our great country, as the motivation for writing *A Compass Pointing West*.

Two poems connected with the family related Home Cemetery, where generations of my father's family and relatives are buried, share a common place. *The Old Home Cemetery* originally appeared in my first book, *Oh God, Where Art Thou? The Great Conundrum*, and *The Caretaker* was written for my brother, Robert. The final three poems are a trilogy, part fiction with small, surgical incisions of real events that follow a family's journey through *Magic in the Trees*, *The Dragon's Lair*, and *The Miracle of the Polished Stone*. The trilogy presents a dynamic illustration of the dichotomy of human consciousness; the Yin and Yang of the circle of reality and fantasy, tragedy and joy, and despair and redemption.

As you read the poems, you may notice the obvious influence of eastern religions, especially Buddhism and Taoism, and the influence of east Asian philosophers such as Mencius, Lao Tzu, and Confucius. Christian, Jewish, and Islamic influences, although less dominate, can be found by those with open and discriminating eyes. Perhaps more obvious is the regard I have and the timeless influence of the Bard, William Shakespeare. Finally, the *process-oriented ethics* philosophy embodied in the writings of Nikos Kazantzakis is an ever-present influence. In the end, I am a person of eclectic tastes and passions for the mysteries of life and the universe we inhabit. Hence, with me there is always the Yin and the Yang, the infinitesimal and the grand, the common and the unique, and the mortal and the eternal that find expression within the lines I write.

A more recent intruder into my thoughts, philosophy, and life is the practice of karate and the Bushido of Japanese samurai. From the samurai I put aside aspects of *the way of the warrior* and admire their code of honor, loyalty, courage, and integrity. From karate, I have gained new insights into the hidden powers of self-discipline, self-reflection, self-confidence, and compassion, charity, and love of nature. Most fascinating to me, beyond the *Hara, Ki, Kime,* and *Kiai,* is Karate's concept of *Mishu.* The loosely translated concept of "mind of no mind" means that ritual practice for years allows the dedicated devotee to act, move, to be without conscious thought to trigger an action, a response, or in the case of the meditator to move from mindfulness to the awakened blissful state of emptiness.

The photo of Alexander McCollum, his wife Mollie, and their son James (my grandfather) was taken by an unknown photographer sometime between 1907 and 1909. Alexander was among the last of the generations of gentlemen farmers and artisan entrepreneurs who lived through the end of the agricultural age, and they saw the demise of their wealth and standing in the community fall prey to a new age of industrialism and the rise of manufacturing, banking, and finance interests. Alexander attended Hiram College, was a member of the City School Board, and, like his father, Ira, was a staunch anti-slavery Republican. Alex, as my father remembered him, was a loyal member of Lincoln's party. Local historian Vince Shivers, working on a project with Youngstown City School students, was never able to confirm rumors that the homestead was involved directly with the underground railroad, but he mentioned to me at the homestead's dedication ceremony as an Ohio historical site that, based upon my family's circle of friends, it was more than probable that they were sympathetic, if not helpful, to others in the area who actively assisted runaway slaves in their perilous journeys to freedom.

I want to thank Joan McCollum Slipski, Jenny McCollum Mills and Charles Mills for their excursions on my behalf into Mill Creek Park to take photos for me that I used as inspirational reminders of the park's innate beauty. The photos of Mill Creek Park and Idora Park in decay were taken by my son, Eric James McCollum, with me as his fretful accomplice. Finally, I took the photo of the Wantanabi spirit talking stick; a family heirloom that

Preface

Donna, Annemarie, Eric, and I actually painted as a family project before the children were teenagers. The Wantanabi sits against a corner wall in my home office and is a source of daily introspection, inspiration, and affirmation of how precious and wonderful a gift is the life we have and are able to share.

James McCollum
March 2, 2020

Acknowledgements

As I NOTED IN my first book *Oh God, Where Art Thou? The Great Conundrum,* in all that I write, as a poet or otherwise, I have found John Bartlett's encyclopedic *Bartlett's Familiar Quotations,* the background resource it was intended to be, an invaluable tool for helping an author discover and trace passages, phrases, sayings, and proverbs to their original sources. It provides an easy route to discover, or rediscover, the ancient texts, the Bible, the complete works of Shakespeare, and thousands of others. For a writer of fiction, a poet, a practitioner of the lost art of letter writing, this wonderous compilation of wisdom enables the researcher to subsequently go directly to the source and find the inspiration and fuel for the imagination to refashion with new meanings and interpretations, in light of the twenty-first century, age-old wisdom and insight into economic, social, and political conditions, the psychology of the mind, the evolution of scientific discovery, and religious and spiritual insights that have fermented and given birth to heady new vintages of religious and spiritual thought, insight, and criticism.

I am indebted to a college classroom book printed fifty years ago for a refresher on Europe's Age of Exploration. I used Wallace Ferguson and Geoffrey Bruun's *A Survey of European Civilization* in my first Western Civilization class as an undergraduate, and now, nearly fifty years later, it was a helpful resource that resurrected, from my memory banks, the lectures of faculty in Western Civilization and U.S. history survey classes, and especially the lectures of Dr. Leslie Domonkos from upper-division European history courses that I took as an undergraduate at Youngstown State

Acknowledgements

University; all creating a synergy of creative thought in crafting the poem, *A Compass Pointing West.*

Prof. Martha Pallante's paper, "The Trek to Ohio: Early Travel Narratives and Perceptions of the Frontier," was a helpful resource for understanding the challenges settlers faced in the long hard overland slog from the northeast and mid-Atlantic coasts of colonial America to the Ohio Territory. "A History of the Presbyterian Church in Basking Ridge, New Jersey," written by Dorothy Loa McFadden, was a helpful resource in understanding the plight of Scotch rebels and seekers of religious freedom who voluntarily or by royal edit of banishment braved the Atlantic crossing to be among the early immigration wave to a new world in colonial North America. A final resource is the 1834 business journal of Ira McCollum, a resource rich with insight into the economy of the early 1800s in Mahoning County, Ohio. This treasure has been in our family's possession for 185 years. Once *The Old Mill Creek: The Park Collection* is published, my siblings and I intend to donate this historical artifact to Youngstown State Universitys' Maag Library Rare Book Collection for preservation for future generations of scholars and students of Ohio History.

James McCollum

Star-Crossed Lovers, Nevermore

If you dare, then follow along as ten-thousand
crows breach the air with tormented calls
of *nevermore* within a haunting song, a breach of peace—
protesting fate's cruel separations, urgency's desperation,
not unlike Verona's tragedy of woe
of star-crossed lovers' loss of love forevermore.
This story is an ageless one; a winged flight
that spells out triumph against a tyrant's might.
It's an ancient tale mined from iron ore
drawn from deep within the earth's molten core
eons of time before its mysteries—washed by hand
and hung outside to dry—a closed door no more;
blessed with the gift of a seer's discriminating sight
opening graves, and resurrecting dormant bodies, minds,
and souls in the glow of a new day's bright light.
Compositions, cast in metal ingots,
kept intact an aged tongue; a diction lost in time
with few stepping stones from shelf to ascending shelf,
until in a cloud of dust a clue was found
and sequestered messages, natural pearls bound
within their shells, were in a glorious resurrection
energized; sleep's long watch aborted,
as linguists culled the wisdom tracks trapped
within a lexicon of lost lines wandering
frenetically within Pan's labyrinth.
Historians culled paper pages, enough to fell
a Sherwood forest, rolled into library stacks
full of scrolls scholars held out to their robed cult

and declared these are the *Chronicles of Avian*.
Today, that treasure trove is ripe for all who have not,
like a haunting ghost disused through long neglect,
lost the practiced skill to read the written word.
Columned lines, row after row, like swords
held by guards along a fence, flowed flawlessly
from calligrapher's pens dipped in the indigo ink
of an ancient, vanished *Scribner's* guild.
The six-fingered ones were a rare breed,
unique as their sister and brother shamans
who relied on spoken words and did not write
the messages they saw and spoke of in visions
of the scary night—the painted signs inside
Neanderthal caves depicting spirits of the dead
whom they called upon for intervention in the hunt
for meat, fish, and foul, and berries found on plants
as seasons changed with spring and summer's heat.
Through windows into cloistered monastic cells,
nature's light, the sun and moon, gave feeble
sight to pages the six-fingered writer's cult
slaved on day and night by candle light,
preserving an ancient culture's myths, folklore,
legends, and the fabled lessons they foretold;
all waiting patiently for the long-neglected opportunity
for freedom's call to ring and rhythmic lines
to breach the ground so, words too long unsaid
could breathe the air and give an eerie voice
to a resurrection chorus led by ancestral ghosts
freed from the spirit lands to which their souls
held traveling passes enabling them to intercede,
to reconnect with earth's elements.
In transcribed scrolls, the Scribner's Guild
chronicled the times that followed three-hundred-
million years of dinosaur kings that ruled
the earth until the great fire of extinction
flamed, and in its wake brought on the cruel,

precipitous demise of the Mesozoic era's
giant reptile kings, and much later birthed
a new era of smaller mammals and human-kind's
remarkable but rather unlikely, fragile rise.
This, we know with an uncertain assurance,
for the scribes, who lay claims to an inner sight
within their dreams, have in writing told us so.
And, then, more and more came the tales
of great winged lizards with orange-flamed
fire breath, stoked from furnace kilns
deep within their armor-plated shells.
Each beast's belly held a fire rock
unleashed from the sky above, a giant orb
crashing thoughtlessly into a helpless,
unaccepting sea. And in the sea-god's anger,
in retribution for the fiery intrusion,
Poseidon spewed molten rocks skyward
across the planet earth, bringing night's
long death in clouds of sulfur dust that rode
the airwave currents like a wild herd
of dark, red-eyed horses Satan summoned
from scorched fields that marked the burnt out
upper rings of Hade's black-holed well,
where God before said they must forever dwell.
It was a time, too, when other feathered
flying things, birds we humans came to call,
were prisoners of a dragon master ghoul,
a self-proclaimed protector of his realm.
Gregore, with a hard first *e* which means
great gorge of molten ore in Avian, was expelled
from the spacious cleft in the hard earth's
crust, the last of its kind to burst free
from Mother Earth's reluctant womb
as tectonic plates clashed and butting
heads closed the rift and opening
never more for Avian eyes to see.

For a thousand times a thousand years
Gregore the Great ruled supreme,
a guardian gargoyle, an oleaginous uncouth
king, who through forced labor, stone
by tiny stone, carried in small birds' beaks
built a wall so high and far that no small
feathered flying thing could freely sail
in flight beyond the lair of the dragon king,
or enter from outside without a fiery fate
that spilled out in certain death, as sure
as Elizabeth's warning, if Spain's armada
in a fool's rush invade her island realm.
The kingdom of the reptile of the sky
branched out in giant circles from its center
near a ledge of jutting stone looking down
on the falling waters that poured quickly
over and down Lanterman's Falls within
the gorge carved out of the Old Mill Creek.
It's there, in the center of its kingdom—
a pulsing heart vibrating outward in ever-
increasing rings of concentric circles—
where the self-possessed winged reptile
king returned each day to roost and rest.
Sly beast, it was, that never fell into
a deep, uninterrupted sleep; always,
only apparently asleep, its eyes were open
through thin slits, its ears cupped like satellite
cones, its nose attuned like sharks to water
with tainted blood, were its sensory tools
on vigilant alert that no one dare take leave
of their sovereign liege, nor enter from beyond
the wall into the great winged lizard's lair
without a pledge of life-long fealty to the dragon
overlord, who without the Scribner's unwitting aid
would have passed forlorn and forgotten,
a complete unknown in the annals of history.

Thus, in tribute and with a prisoner's fear,
all subjects of his realm were required to hail
and bow to the power and glory of Gregore
the Great, the armor-plated beast smelt from iron
ore long before the advent of two-legged creatures
bound to earth with their recalcitrant, unsure feet.
Each day the dragon lord would rise and across
his kingdom fly, each circle doubling nine times
out toward the great wall's end, far from the falls
beside Lanterman's outcropped rock ledge
the embittered dragon chose as its royal seat.
The scaled beast's realm stretched northeast
to a great shallow lake, west to flat plains
of wheat, to the south to a river's long snaking
course, and last to a round-topped mountain range
that slowly rose in gradual heights heading east.
Once in a lunar cycle, when the moon
was about to fully bloom, the fire-breathing
ogre would scorch the ground nearest the wall
of all its vegetation and leave a barren landscape
where no one, big or small, could hide
from the jealous eyes of the dragon beast.
Despite the dragon's ritual flaming purge,
wild flowers, like their sister bees—essential
to most living things above the seas—did not
fade away. The flowers' beauty, a fanciful delight
until the full approach of the dreaded moon
and the doom it meant to flowers on the glorious
cusp of a burst of brilliant color in full bloom.
"Damned flowers," Gregore would say,
"these wild flowers are not heaven sent to me."
And in the midst of this patch of scorched earth,
where wild flowers died and were reborn,
lay burnt bones and charred skeletal remains
of defiant birds who dared challenge the law
declared by the lord of the Old Mill Creek.

The Chronicles say a century passed,
or more, since the last freedom-seeking
Avian sought to fly away to lands beyond
the lethal barrier. Gregore, the horrible,
made deadly sure that no one could forget
enchantment's exacting cost, the heavy penalty
borne by all who defied the mighty overlord.
No one rankled the sneering beast more
than *Gniroas*, pronounced with emphasis
on the letter "n" and with a silent *G*, that deftly
translated in Avian meant *soaring to the clouds*.
Each day while the dragon took to the sky,
the white-crowned eagle would soar like souls
that rise into the clouds, then glide in a steep
rapid descending dive toward the wall.
And each day, old fire breath would watch
and wait from within the clouds, its eyes
set for the eagle to make one fatal mistake
and fly to breach the master's high stone stall.
Gregore would stoke and fire up the hot rock
smoldering in his belly pot to a blacksmith's
heated hearth and smoke would start to leak
from its nostrils and fire lick its lips
when the mocking eagle would halt its soaring
glide within a single wingspan of the grim wall's
dark inside; just before old iron side was armed
and ready to toast its most annoying nemesis
with a fire-roasting burst of flame, a flame
so hot with self-loathing hate that even God
within a burning bush would be consumed.
Gniroas would swiftly turn away, look
skyward toward the clouds, stare into
the mighty dragon lord's tense cursing eyes,
and he would see Gregore, in frustration,
shake its head, cool down the heated rock,
and foiled, snort out an impotent puff of smoke.

You see, it was the dragon master's own code
of established law, that no one died until
they were within a crow's beak from breaching
his damned, abominable, despairing wall.
There came a time when two sparrows,
enamored in love's early dawn, flirted
with each other on a hillside crest below
the lower peaks of the mountain range
that slowly rose up from the eastern wall.
As they gazed down, their sharp eyes
could see a bed of wild flowers; tantalizing,
standing out like the apples Adam eyed.
Dinnione, pronounced with a silent *e*
missing from her name, that means *a jeweled
diamond* in Avian, the female of the two,
said to her lover *Solastar*, the *S* silent
to start his name with Avian emphasis placed
on a beginning *o*, meaning *to fly among the stars*:
"Aren't those wild flowers—filled with colors
soft and comforting—beautiful, but cruelly
out of place inside that ugly, foreboding wall?"
Solastar nodded his agreement, then told Dinnione
to stay quiet while he would leave her for
a moment, as short as most bird's dreams,
to gather in his beak this sweet unfolding day
a fresh bouquet of wild flowers for his love.
Despite her protests that he should not cross over
to the flowers within the wall, he knew he had
to do so, for tomorrow by his best reckoning
was the night of the full moon, the dreaded day
that Gregore chose to scorch the earth nearest
the inside of the wall and it would take weeks
before more flowers would repopulate
the soil that time and fire had burned, and as seasons
turned became a rich, dark, fertile earthy birthing loom.
Determined to impress his love and secure

a cherished gift, Solastar did not hear Dinnione's
halting plea to wait, for he was wrong, she reasoned—
today, by her recollection foretold a full moon.
Driven like the wind howling through the gorge
of the Old Mill Creek, Solastar sailed by love
possessed, oblivious to the danger lurking
in the clouds, into the dragon king's captive land.
All the while, Gregore watched the drama unfold,
and set his mind in stone to turn an innocent
misfortune into a tragedy that would sadly
be told and retold and serve his purposes to impose
his will upon the subjects Phaedo said have no cause
or right to open prison doors and run away.
Solastar dove from the top of the wall down
to the wild flowers bunched and gathered
in a natural rainbow bed, unaware the winged
lizard beast, in a deeper dive from high within
the cloudy sky, was trying to decide if a puny-sized
intruder should die, or simply bleed red,
and live, miserably inside, forevermore.
Gregore chose the latter out of cruelty,
keeping Solastar alive but captive, separated
by fear of death for his missing mate,
the feathered beauty, Dinnione, whose song
of tears Solastar, from across the wall,
would in anguished pain daily hear.
But the dragon's ego never opened its
jealous eyes to a truth that the distance
separating desire from unrecoverable despair
was a leap the gallant bird could some
day find clever means to navigate.
Hope, he acknowledged, would not swiftly come
to rescue him from cruel fate's twisted curse.
But Solastar knew from the center of his core
that without hope, as grapes deprived of sun
and water would yield no harvest wine, love

would wither in such a famine and die
a tortured death upon a shriveled vine.
While the dragon landed thunderously
beside the tiny bird that held within its beak
a batch of flowers from the wild bed
that it had picked for his dear love,
an eagle passed by overhead in a glide
taking him to the top of the wall, a place
where oblivion waits patiently for all to cross
into another realm; to stumble or sail no concern
to the blind eyes of the keeper of the night.
Then just before, in the soaring height
of a daily feigned ritual, the clever mocking
bird of prey turned away, pulled up fast
in straight flight, found a strong wind current
and rode it hard like a rushing cresting wave.
Off within the wind, came an annoying
sightless sound the jealous dragon heard
each day in its conditioned memory.
The eagle's flight, its passing sight and sound,
an old familiar object in the sky, as dawn bears
witness once each day, the dragon without lapse
or pause never failed to catalog annoyance
and charge a credit to its iron memory bank.
And the sly eagle, who always had the aura
of certainty in the pitch of its leashed flight,
flew back home to a cold and empty nest
atop an ancient oak that had grown from
a small shoot that burst free from the forest
floor below some four-hundred years ago,
to gaze upon its universe and through
that opening the sun and moon it loves.
The enormous tree thrived along a traveled
earthen trail, Goliath within a green army
of conifers with cones and other friends
that grow and shed green leaves, all following

the winding course of the Old Mill Creek.
"Within these walls I am a worshiped god,"
Gregore was fond to say, "I, and I alone,
decide divine providence, I am the arbiter
of fate, the one who tolls the time and day."
Fear was Gregore's currency. It was the tribute
it exacted; for no matter how weary living
prisoner's lives may be, it pales to desperate
thought within unsettled minds accosted
with the specter of dying and the dead.
But one bird of prey, with tenacious hope
its Spartan core, in resilience and in stealth,
would not surrender salvation's holy grail.
Gniroas would not bow or be bound
to a cruel obedience to gods or despots'
hidden will. There is, he recognized,
a dark malice within the soulless beast,
trapped in an egoist's haughty terror,
that reaps punishments in savage retribution
upon a world it fears full of plots and mutiny.
The eagle knew in full measure the dragon's
arrogance of character; for trapped within
the despot's bluster was a coward undercover,
and every day its throne was cast aside in dire
images of conspiracies hatched by legions
of enemies seeking justice too long delayed
for a cruel tyrant, no just god, in mercy
for crimes against a species, could forgive.
Before the sun would slowly rise, when birds
would start their songs and sounds of instruments
with strings greet the dawning day, two lovers'
daily symphony of pain played out to a full
orchestra, while the conductor of the opera of woe,
his cruel wand in hand, felt no shame or penitence.
The eagle heard the sweet song strung on honeyed
strands; lost love remembered through each sad

and tortured day, and thought to himself
in a grief he could not abate:
Who is this beast, what profane right has it
that separates lovers from their missing love?
Why are they among the crucified, like I,
the absent one, who was away, bound toward
the northern lake, not near enough to help
when a child first took to dangerous flight
and its mother, with feathered wings
spread out, its flushed heart in panic mode,
assaulted by a parent's greatest fear,
flew into death's dark face, in a futile
fiery sacrifice to rescue a child too soon
to leave the safety of its birthing nest?
Homer wrote that the gods have given talents
different to each man. If the *Iliad* rings true,
then one among those gifts was the beauty
of the melody of a lyre and song released
for waiting ears to hear and souls to touch.
Such was the melancholy song, a song
of thwarted love purloined, that Gniroas
heard from sweet Dinnione; like Helen's lips,
it nearly freed his wounded soul from deep
within the cavern to which it was consigned.
Each mournful day until her voice was strained
and rendered still, she called out to Solastar;
and never once did her love denied grow cold
for him whom she could not cuddle, hug, or hold.
Compassion was not nature's gift to birds of prey,
but the lonely eagle of the Old Mill Creek
was moved in pity by the small bird's cruel fate.
The eagle was a silent witness that the layered stones
of the high imposing wall could not hold fast
to their coerced purpose to keep love out.
He heard the stones, awake to the sparrow's
desperate song, cry out in protest from their prison

wall, "We are all victims of a crime most foul."
Gniroas' kind were born to war, with instincts
that presage the time of the samurai, and codes
of honor, loyalty, and courage in the moment,
and a karma in their fates that catapult proud
warriors to another life. Undaunted, the best
that Avian has to give, stare without quarter
into the rapture, and charge headlong into battle
like a cresting wave rushing to a lonely death.
The law within the walls that Gregore ruled
declared a grievous crime to kill another
living thing that has wings that ride upon the air,
so, birds of prey and crows, sparrows, all feathered
creatures within the realm did no harm to one another.
Oh, don't applaud the dragon beast, for what might
on the surface seem like an act of benevolence.
Do not forget this law did not apply to him.
It was up to Gregore's whim who lives, who dies
within the walls that trap its captive subjects
in that prison of incarcerated innocents.
And the budding flower of sparrow love,
once blessed with spring's fresh breath
of rain-soaked air and summer's warmth,
held fast in the faith of graceful swans
paired for life. Their anchored faith
spoke in a whispered hush, "When next
we meet, destiny's love will not have died,
and we will fly free of the dragon beast."
Seasons passed like water tumbling over
Lanterman's Falls. The sparse talk between
Gniroas and Solastar, once forced, gave way
to frequent conversations as friendship deepened
like new wine aged patiently. In measured time,
the unfamiliar acquaintances would pull the cork,
and together they would taste and savor
the best that fermented grapes are born to give.

The eagle was the quieter of the two and
not inclined toward a quantity of words.
Mercy was the gift he gave to his tortured
friend, who craved one set of ears to hear,
one soul to feel his pain that heaven's gates
were closed by a fallen angel's maliciousness
and kept him from his sweet love, Dinnione.
"Can God not bear witness to my suffering
from heaven's lofty perch? I look skyward
to heaven's portal, the glowing sun, but find
no succor, no answer to when my love and I,
a love divided by that vile cursed wall,
shall ever meet again, ever soar with wings
on wind, and side by loyal side fly away."
Gniroas' firm rebuke was softened
with good intent: "Do not entertain such bad
thoughts, they are poison to your mind.
Though your thoughts turn desperate, more
desperate than the tongues of wild dogs lapping
in a carrion feast, the time is not quite right,
not opportune for a love impaired to be renewed."
Comfort stood beyond the moment's grasp;
for Solastar the stars that populate night's sky
seemed closer at hand and easier to reach.
"What cruel choice have I, to live this life
immune to death within these walls, banished
from the mate with whom my soul connects,
or concede to suicide and fly to the top
of the wall and incur a certain fiery death?"
The eagle's response came quickly,
swift as Montague's sharpened sword's
fatal thrust into a Capulet's startled flesh.
"Do not rush like a madman headlong
into the glowing firmament. Recuse
yourself from pity while you still live;
save breath, for flight and love, rare

possibilities, remain to be obtained.
If you are still and do not move, the muddy
water in the Lily Pond we fly by each day
will slowly, with meditation's seeing eyes,
clear for you to peer into its murky depths.
The dragon is a beast, and craven beasts
do not have the lowest coins to parcel
out a share of pity as small as grains of sand."
"My friend, you mistake my receptiveness,"
Solastar replied. "I am exhausted by words
of banished hope. Hope is lost, washed away
like waves crashing into a distant shore.
Please, speak no more, your words hurt
my ears and pain my sickened soul."
Gniroas spread out his wings, a flourish
and a flag embossed in anger. "Then
you are truly mad, and fair love has killed
your soul. Too much the cost of love!"
"Now listen well, open up your ears,
for I will not speak of this again.
I have a plan to best the dragon beast.
You and I, together, may yet fly to ring
the freedom bell, atop the accursed wall,
that all might leave this living hell.
So, hope must endure, that Dinnione,
unlike you, is not entrapped in a web
of gloom and melancholy, and does
not seek relief with her heart pierced
mortally upon a bush of pointed thorns."
As for Dinnione, from her vista on the hill
below the mountains rise, with a bird's
keen sight each day she spied her absent love,
her dearest friend entombed in hell;
and she in limbo, as both poured tears
that fouled the ground as blood does so
upon a battlefield. And all the while,

the two lovers languished in despair,
the joy of love triumphant contradicted
and entrance to heaven's bliss constricted
by fortune's fickle master of the wheel of time.
Each day, a weary Solastar raised his banner,
tattered wings of molted feathers, as a flout
to the dragon beast who rules the sky
and land below, and a signal to his love
beyond the unjust wall that he was there
for her to see and for him to hear from her
a warbled song of days that turn to years
and pain that yearns for absent love's return.
And Dinnione, a melancholy poison encroaching
on her peace of mind, was pricked with thoughts
of death's dark contagion and bemoaned the beast
whose envy thwarts loves best intents.
Hers was a most unnatural utterance for a soul
as sweet as bee's brewed malted honey.
The daily ritual was a play that Gniroas
knew too well, a dream that he could not
in good conscience casually dispel.
No, he thought to himself. *If I have will
and life, then death shall not befall to love
such as that of Dinnione and Solastar.
I will not concede to a cruelty that kills
the flowers of love that are in imperiled bloom.
I cannot delay long to cast aside their gloom,
and set upon a course with Solastar to end
the bond that binds us to captivity, and ends
the songs of praise the warden of wall,
with healing mercy plucked out of its eyes,
covets from the subjects it so dislikes.
I must conjure up a plan to lure the selfish
king into complacency that I can then convey
to Dinnione, but how remains the key to solve?
What if each day on my flight to the top*

of the ghastly wall, I drop a stone
with a feigned angry look as it careens
off the top without disturbing a single
stubborn clinging rock and tumbles safely
to the ground inside, the subtle sound
no clue to the coming call of freedom
from the land beyond the wall, encoded
in a song sang in a dialect the sparrows
share, but is among a few in Avian,
the dragon does not fully comprehend?
Next day, Gniroas said to Solastar,
"I have a plan to charm a snake to sleep,
that's fraught with risk we have to take,
if ever you hope within the tracking
of the seasons of a year to reunite
with your love in summer's bloom."
"Well please be quick, I cannot wait,
talk with me now about this scheme,
for I have reached a reckless point
and shall no longer have the will to dream,"
said Solastar depressed that life, with love
denied could be so harsh and mean.
"Put aside your fear of loss of the love
that your mind cannot tolerate, your dread
of such calamity blocks your path to sanity.
Put down that vessel full of selfish want,
lift up the earthen bowl that is half full
and find satisfaction in a vessel that is not
an empty set to put your mind at ease.
Well then, tomorrow marks a month
until green leaves turn brown, and early
ones are freed to ride a gentle breeze,
without the glum old ferryman, before
they find the waiting ground below.
It's then, we must begin the long deceit,"
said Gniroas, "for it will take the full

turn of the season's wheel to charm
the dragon master into a momentary lull;
and that will be our sole chance to catch
the clever overlord in a moment of neglect.
Gregore's folly is that he labels things and only
sees surfaces that do not penetrate other
living things such as sister's deep call out
to seek and touch their connecting souls.
What comes before, the dragon misapprehends,
does not of necessity compel what follows."
Then day after day, as a mill wheel turns
and grain is ground into flour, Solastar flew
below the eagle dangerously close to a crow's beak
of the bleak depressing wall, then descended
to the wild flower patch, while Gniroas
caught the current of a rushing cresting wave
and soared straight up to just beneath the clouds
where old ironside was sure to daily hide,
before he flew like a bird of prey possessed
back to the empty nest atop the giant oak
that is always first within the Old Mill Creek
to hear and feel the coming of a rising wind.
Together, every day without change in time
or path of flight, the sparrow and the eagle flew
to the wall's foreboding edge; and Gniroas
covered Solastar with the bold feathers
of his outstretched wings, while Solastar
grew in trust of his ally in the sky above,
as the sparrow flew within the shadows
underneath the eagle's outspread wings.
Each bird within its talons held a stone
released the moment they came closest
to the top of the wall. Gniroas' gnarled stone
never seemed to damage the mortar fastening
the stones of the wall in place, as Solaster's
small pebbles, more clever than a serpent, fell

harmlessly as a dove to the ground outside.
The dragon shook his head, high within
the clouds in mocking disgust and thought
to his single-minded self, *Silly birds will never*
dent my wall with the fleckless things the fools
have chosen to drop against my great barrier;
a shield that has stood defiantly in the face of time,
a heap of stones bearing witness to the dashed hopes
that died in a bloody sea of dreadful deaths nearby.
Each day, as monks rise to sing at morning
services, the birds, too, took to their daily rituals
as fall's colors faded to winter's raiment of nature's
whitest snow that gives birth to spring, the season-
lover's dream of while trapped in winter's chill.
Gregore, the dragon overlord, so careful
on his watch, passed from annoyance
to boredom and indifference to the duo's
futile efforts to ruin his cherished wall.
He never saw or pieced together the strategy
the birds had hatched. He did not apprehend
that the small pebbles Solastar dropped
and always missed the wall, while Gniroas'
larger stones bounced back without a dent
to evidence its assault, were in fact coded
messages from Solastar to Dinnione to hold
him in her heart for he would soon flee to safety
and the shadows that haunt her days would flee
with spring rains when summer comes to bloom.
So, Dinnione would casually land near
the wall outside and scratch the ground
for tiny crawling things to eat while carefully
discovering Solastar's secret messages of hope
and dear love not lost, just in complicated
cruel delay. She reassured herself with thoughts
that pain and suffering are attendants to this life,
but also heighten the joy of gentle kindness,

benevolence, grace, civility, and compassion,
and the heady passions heaven pairs with love.
"This is our day, my dear small friend,
it is now or never for our perilous endeavor,"
said Gniroas to his tiny charge. "I have allies
who will aid our cause. Now is the time to lose
all fears you have of a violent death. Prepare
to bear your birthright proudly, for today
we will no longer yield to oppression; today,
we launch our attack to ring freedom's bell."
Solastar, his heart swelled with a warrior's
steely purpose replied, "Then let's discharge
our duty, sail upon the buoying air in brave
defiance of injustice long endured to victory
or defeat with honor and committed courage
in the certain face of a challenged god whose
ferocious rage will rise to swallow all that lives,
and walks or crawls upon the ground below."
Gregore was distracted by the cawing
of a restless flock of chattering crows,
and paid no mind to the ritual practice
of the eagle and the sparrow flying toward
his tarnished wall of woe. *I have no time
for such annoyances while other birds
are acting strangely out of character
and demand my full attention to stop
the clamor rising in their noise,* thought
the miscalculating, distracted dragon to itself.
And in that careless moment of distraction,
Gregore did not see the eagle and the sparrow
veer from their normal course as they both
flew over the wall to face a rising sun,
unaware if their fate was couched in a safe
landing or to crash into the shinning orb
and burn in a burst of an angered god's
vengeful, unforgiving searing flame.

The Old Mill Creek

Too late, Gregore realized the birds
he denigrated as fools had breached
his wall and reached the outside unharmed.
Enraged, he recognized he had been duped,
and while his kiln was stoked so high that heat
was now his silent foe, he rushed in flight
too late to stop the scheming birds from
reaching liberty beyond its greedy grasp.
"Foul fowl," he screamed, "you dare abandon
me," he asked in dreadful misbelief, oblivious
to the rising temperature that was about to burst
the pot within his belly, a conflagration his mind
in its twisted strain would forever regret.
Just before his belly burst from inside out,
the dragon, in agony self-imposed, heard
the sound of an approaching airborne army
of ten-thousand screeching crows, a storm
about to pass and scale the endangered wall.
Heat as hot as an exploding star escaped
the armored shell of Gregore the Great;
a fiery pulse that pushed against the wall
while the vibrations of the frantic caws
of fleeing crows shook the stones within
the wall like the trumpets that would later
sound the fall of the wall in Jericho.
The wounded lizard king looked aghast,
as its once invincible barrier grumbled
to the ground and left a circle of rubble
that time's rains would wash away from history.
The dragon, in the throes of defeat, looked
upon the eagle and the sparrow lovers who
had yet to fly away like the crows who
in feverish flight were far out of sight.
The absent lovers, now reunited, bowed
in gratitude to their eagle friend, then looked
with undeserved pity toward the wounded dragon

and flew away toward the low-lying mountains
rising to the east, nevermore to turn around.
Gregore in pain that penetrated to its core
said to Gniroas in a state of disbelief,
"Look what you have done. You have ruined
everything. Within my wall you were safe
from harm and could live with me in peace."
"You still do not understand," was Gniroas'
sad response. "Your freedom from the pangs
of death comes with a price too high to pay.
For your grace we gave away our liberty;
we were captive, slaves to your grand design.
We were not the masters of our own bliss.
We choose freedom even if that means
chaos, death, and a journey to whatever portal
opens next, even it if its only labor's rest."
The dragon turned its head as Gniroas flew away;
the eagle's fading screech calling freedom's name.
Gregore, impaired in flight, returned to Lanterman's
ledge and drank all the water that pooled below
the falls before it crawled inside the cave above,
coughed up the once hot rock that had cooled,
and turned into a small egg-shaped piece
of pure polished obsidian. It was its final act
before it died and its body turned to stone and
its eyes to emerald green before they closed.
It was its seeming final act before, like
all living things, returning to its roots.
And at that moment the doves of peace
were finally free to roost on tree tops and
eventually on roof tops of homes wherever
they may be; and the once star-crossed lovers,
Dinnione and Solastar, too were free to make
their way without a promise of what fate might
hold within the cards that living things receive
from a shuffled deck of possibilities.

This is their new reality; they are no longer
prisoners to another's will. They are free,
no longer condemned to stay without
the choice to fly away; to taste and savor
the best of love's labor; to reach for happiness
in the quest for God's wisdom—all the earth's
riches as free as wind and water and fire;
to seek the truth inscribed within creation's
dawning moment; to confront destiny's random,
careless chaos with charity and compassion—
as Samaritans who see and help the homeless
and the hungry they pass along the way;
to escape the cruel pain and suffering that traps
all conscious beings upon the circling miller's wheel,
but leaves the tiny birds unshackled, free at last,
free to find their bliss in moments of awakened joy.

The Rose

It was a long and leisurely walk,
I often took on summer days,
along the weathered earthen trail
that meanders through an urban park
filled with trees and wild flowers,
streams, ponds, and lakes, and rocky
outcrops of ancient monolithic stones
that line and guard the roads
twisting through the gorge nature sculped
patiently millions of years ago.
It's a spiritual place, a magical forest,
my father, with childlike reverence called
the Old Mill Creek until his dying day.
As a youngster wandering along its trails,
all that I experienced, inorganic and alive,
somehow seemed connected, touching, seeing,
hearing, smelling creation's mystery in that park.
I never ceased to be amazed, nor was my wonder
ever grander, than coming upon a random
patch of wild flowers; a multicolored palette
that nature placed before my eyes, a natural
beauty no master's brush could ever replicate.
More wonderous still was the rose
I once saw; a single crimson crown
caught up within a sea of wind tossed,
tangled, ragged weeds born with ill intention
to choke the life within an errant flower
that foolishly intrudes into its realm.

Now, my mind, ripened in experience,
bursts free. Enlightened, I am no longer
a prisoner in the dark, trapped within,
confined, unseeing in convention's chains.
I feel and sense the strings vibrate faintly,
and span across the universe. Their quiver
touching every moment, everything;
a harmonious testament to knowledge's limits
to the brace of experience's eyes and ears.
Now, I understand the truth of beauty;
unhidden and unobscured, plainly
the rose was not an accidental aberration.
The single regal flower crowned in nature's
potent possibilities grew to stand alone;
its grand, inherent worth born to blossom
in its native beauty. The thorn-stemmed
rose did battle with the weeds and despite
appearance was not a captive in a foreign land.
I salute this rose, as it defied the limits
the weeds so foolishly sought to impose.
The rose, you see, is my hero;
a firm redress to false fortunes' fools.

A Compass Pointing West

How was it that two families converged
and in their merger came to me as one?
This true story, similar to the paths of
other family journeys, follows a river's
lengthy twisted course from its original source
on to the sea's awaiting, welcoming estuary.
The families came from a common land;
a fretful band of men and women and children,
too, who journeyed across an ocean, not calm
so that lambs might lay in peace with placid
wolves, but with rough seas and winds that tore
at ship's sails and shook its captive passengers
to their huddled, soggy, trembling core.
They came, these foreigners, as searchers
to find new lives and build new homes
in frontier land nearby the Old Mill Creek.
The gods of ages set a challenge to Adonis,
and set aside an island bed of wild flowers
where good women and men could cast aside
sluggish senses, and their souls would be freed,
blessed to be among ones who might rush to open
shuttered blinds and see another side of nature
and its mysterious creative, unnamed source divine;
a glimpse into the One that stands alone,
defies time, and is immune to simple definitions
other than vague insights drawn from intuitions.
This dream, America's dream, cannot be told
without first searching into history's vast archives;

to sift through ancestral roots, to find a source,
discover the origins of honored family crests,
such as *in ardua petit*; which roughly translated
means, "He has attempted many difficult things."
The crest of *in ardua petit* once waved in wild
Scottish winds, a brandished flourish in the district
of Lorn in Argyll, on the banks of Loch Avich,
on ancient land near the northwest highland coast;
a fief granted by Sir Duncan Campbell in 1414,
in gratitude for loyalty and a defender's support,
to the faithful chieftain of the Malcom Clan.
For now, I beg your patient understanding,
for it will take many lines to distill the malted
history of two blended journeys to the sacred ground
of the green canopied forest of the Old Mill Creek.
Close your eyes, set your backs straight, and take
a deep breath. Return to the Golden Age of Exploration
and the grand games among European thrones,
where actors entertained paying customers
in scenes upon a wooden stage in Shakespeare's
plays, portraying the vain ambitions of Europe's
peevish royalty—underlings, assuredly, in the minds
of the winged legions that guard the gates of Eden,
where petty man is now forever banished,
a plague upon God's garden, a deadly carcinogen.
Kings and queens, princesses and princes
alike never braved, never had to fear
the cold Atlantic crossings their subjects,
willingly or forcibly conscripted, had to endure.
The sea, you see, is central to this history;
and on that boundless water way, a small
device turned out to be the savior of many
an intrepid captain's questionable integrity.
The stars in all their majesty could not
a captain's counselor be, and ships would pass
in circles captively but for the tiny needle

of a sailor's compass pointing the way
toward a queen or king's frantic search on soil
foreign to their kingdoms that loomed across
a salted sea as vast as heaven's casting net;
a mesh of twisted, silken strands that blankets
humankind in foggy dreams of grandeur,
granting no rest or quarter to minds obsessively
inhospitable to illusion's barren handmaiden.
And here, the challenge lies: Can you construct
a credible counterpoint to the fact that what humans
perceive as authentic and indisputable is mostly based
on faith, and a faith alone that pushes reason aside
in the manic quest to understand reality, if with rational
allowance, we can assert that reality is real at all?
"There are New Worlds," their overwrought
explorers said, "Majesty, that are treasure filled,
for those bold enough to seize fate's openings
to good fortunes' greatest opportunities."
But royal greed was blind, dull to a world
hardly new. No noble saw or cared to recognize
cultures imbued with a full and ripened past,
alive with customs and traditions centuries long;
long in teeth, longer than a saber tiger's
great, curved, protruding, upper-canine teeth.
People to the east and west had norms and mores
that were exotic and peculiar to self-absorbed
European eyes. Their histories vibrant long before
the west of Europe was little more than a wilderness,
a distant lodging post of Rome—no place Europe's
novice rulers, with the bragging bray of an ass's tongue,
could boast of as their crown, the honored throne
that God above bestowed on them as a royal home.
Petty kings and queens, these guileless neophytes,
compared to nature's primal force, Olympus born,
where the gods of heaven toss thunderbolts across
the sky and the mountains on the earth below are split

apart as avalanches of broken rock roll down
and cover civilizations for long millennia
before they are found, reclaimed by scholars'
baring streets and structures buried underneath.
So short, the clouds of night that hide the ascending
dawn of a new day from sleeping human eyes,
as once great and mighty empires teeter and decline.
The ships of Portugal's compasses pointed to the east,
toward a Bengal tiger snared on a tangled leash.
The Portuguese came to India, to the western coast
of Malabar, where Buddhist monks in Pali
penned sacred scriptures that called upon men
to rise above and do no evil where they lived.
The monk's sacred texts adorned with Asia's
cautious elephants, their thunderous feet walking
carefully about earth's grasslands and forests—
protectorate of the nursing mother who exhales
life's pure elixir into the gods' grandest gift
of our lonely planet's precious atmosphere.
Oh, yes, this is the same India where Kipling
was in Mumbai born, and later wrote enchantingly
in his masterpiece *The Jungle Book* of the young boy,
Mowgli, raised in a jungle den of protective wolves,
while the wolf-boy's mortal enemy, the vengeful tiger,
Shere Khan, was imprisoned in a coat of stripes,
condemned to a life consumed with toxic hate.
Then on they went to the Malay islands, to the China
coast and farther east to the islands of Japan, lying
to the east in the China Sea, where ships were guided
in their search by compasses pointing northeast,
while ship captains feigned confidence that skies
would clear at night, to reveal the constellations
of northern stars whose nightlights calmed thoughts
of dark despair of worried sailors who truly feared
if the watchman's shout out of "land ho" was much
longer delayed, then they would surely find oblivion

in a misty, thunderous plunge at the world's edge,
gone forever over the ledge of an angry vengeful sea.
These royal sanctioned explorers' goals were framed
in a guise of trade. Conquest, they understood to be
a fool's errand as China and Japan, with circumstances
dissimilar from the chaos rife in India with pernicious,
rigid prejudicial castes and religious jealousies crueler
than a pauper's grave, were realistically not candidates
suitable to be conquered or weak enough to be ensnared
in the webs of spiders armed with a thousand eyes that spy
on prey they intend with subterfuge to trap and slay.
The traders and the missionaries of Portugal
were, to most Asians, a dirty, suspicious lot,
more dangerous than a wild dog, beasts
whose guilty minds could not effectively hide
salacious larceny sown in corruption's infamy.
This motely band of Portuguese explorers ventured
east, and to history's judgment their greedy
fingernails, uncleansed, with bloody claws
besmirched from ripping beating hearts within
the hefty flesh of unsuspecting victims, dipped
into the holy water complicit priests blessed
in daily rituals—a tainted, sinful liquid basin
that failed miserably to pass God's absolving test.
The Japanese, especially, saw the lecherous ghost
that lurked behind the curtain; an inner sense
penetrating as deep into Europeans' souls
and motivations as a Samurai's katana out
and on the ready to be thrust into enemies
awaiting flesh, the victim's heart rising
to its throat, coating its gasping mouth dry
with the powder keg of dread and certain coming
death, by painful, piercing inches practiced ritually
a thousand times to breach an enemy's imperiled flesh.
The islands' overlords soon grew hostile to contacts
from these foreigners, and quickly came to realize

the missionaries and traders had no virtuous intent
nor honor in interests other than greed; their unsolicited
visit a surreptitious foil to more sinister motivations
to exploit the native population and spread the pox
of the Jesuits' western creed of Christianity
to Asian souls with a karma that did not seek
or want a place in God's heaven or the Devil's hell.
The warrior class within Japan, imbued with ancestral
honor, tested loyalty, and courage as strong
as the hammered steel of their favored swords,
a courage friends and foes alike extolled,
despised the unarmed barbarians—common beasts
in disdain and slang, they called Gaijin.
In an action of finality, the Shogun lords
and samurai warriors, with razor sharpened katanas
and daggers in their hands, and faces covered
in ferocious beastly masks, consumed with a need
to bring honor to their ancestors, were the force
of Japan that expelled the robed and sandaled
ecclesiastical missionaries and profit-minded traders.
Incensed, Japan's warrior class closed the shores
of the islands of the Rising Sun to the noxious intruders
whose foul presence was an affronting stench
to the islands' checkered groves and cherry-blossom air.
Spain's explorers were a different breed of predators,
not content with mere commercial or religious trade,
the Spaniards armed for war looked to the Americas
with conquest and exploitation on their minds.
Drunk on royal ambition's brew, Spain's tack
was aggressive, a sordid blemished policy of outright
thievery and violence advanced by an army of zealous
clerics and conquistadors; crusaders of another
time who would in false conscience cringe at crimes
of manslaughter or murder thoughtfully done, yet
did not see their own depravity when the slaughter
of a race seemed to them routine, inane,

a trifling matter, no concern to righteous men,
neither cruel, nor to their consciences profane.
The Americas to the south were claimed by roaming
ship born bands of Portuguese and Spaniards;
Brazil was Portugal's to conquer and exploit,
while Peru to Spanish liens was claimed.
But enterprising Spain also paid homage to the north
with Spanish eyes trained on gold and silver mines
in Mexico; to Venezuela and the islands off its coast;
to the southward parts of the territories of Florida
and the southern tier of California's gold rush claims
where yellow sunflower fields painted the coastal landscape
on a canvas crafted by a master's strokes that ushered
in the early arrival of sweet, springtime blooms.
In time, the Spaniard's subterfuge of the islands
waned for the lure of more lucrative gains gleaned
from silver and gold to be reaped from the mainland's
exaggerated treasure troves. But island crops of sugar
and tobacco did not merely disappear. An illicit,
unholy trade was sustained on large colonial estates
by black slaves' lives and labors, and their children's
inheritance too, sold into slavery that greedy men
of European means might see their commercial interests
increase and prosper on the sweat and perspiration
of black-skinned sisters and brothers bought
and bartered for in a spurious human trafficking trade,
exchanged for barrels of island rum produced
on plantation estates from island-harvested sugar cane.
Oh, but early come meant early go to Spanish
and Portuguese superiority. The Dutch, the English,
and the French, in fruitless searches for a northern
passage to the east, gave up that icy arctic quest
and sent emigrants to colonize lands
in the Americas' north, lands void
of serious claims from imperial Spain.
For these European countries, and imperialists

that may follow, the wheels of time turn slow,
for empires such as these, like Rome,
are not built within a single slavish day.
But before their ships sailed west, the Dutch
and English, like the Portuguese and Spaniards
before, looked with sumptuous appetites
toward the inexplicable, exotic Asian east.
The fleets of the Netherlands skirted
around Africa's northeast coast, past
the continent that is the birthing place
of humankind, humanity's common ground,
and set in place the stock company of Dutch
East India in islands known for spice,
an Indonesian treasure grove of nutmeg trees
and crops of cloves; an off-shore business
enterprise the Dutch, true to the operating mode
of corporations of a multinational character,
could manage and control far from home.
The English, for their part, set upon a course
with a subjugated India in its sights and formed
its own East India Company to entrench
British colonial interests on a vast,
fractious, disjointed Indian subcontinent.
English diplomats were dispatched with a royal
strategy to outmaneuver Dutch competitors,
subdue the fragmented princely states and pave
the way for the British empire's occupation,
it's outright illegal subjugation of an entire
subcontinent's teeming population; a rolling sea
of humanity that at the time lacked God's will
to resist, until Gandhi later came and ignited
a glorious revolution with a human quilt
linked thread to thread to the high principles
of resistance to unjust laws, denying a despot's
power through the mantel of human courage
freed of revenge's ferocity, compelled by the might

of righteous indignation and an army trained
in the patient art of peaceful, civil disobedience.
Meanwhile, once entrenched, the archetype,
the colossal of colonialism, subdued the sleeping
dragon whose wings by force the British clipped,
so, for a time India could not fly or fight.
Its long stay in India, skewed English designs
and colored the expectations of the goliath
of unrestrained colonialism that marked a scarlet
letter on Europe's epic Golden Age of Exploration.
But English might could not envision, and did not
within its inner mirror see vanity's quicksand waiting
west in North America's Colonies; and a Parliament
too self-absorbed in superiority ignored Burke's warning
that force by itself can only subdue people temporarily.
The aristocrats had shuttered eyes that did not see,
nor care to understand, that time for gods is tolled
differently than time for downtrodden men.
The British did not heed the warning inscribed
within the psalms that tyranny does not seem to hear—
people may endure sadness and weeping for a long night,
but in the light of the morning sun, joy with unleashed
passion will surely come, and a sleeping dragon
slowly roused to life, in righteous anger rising up,
will to all tyrants be a fearsome scary sight.
While another dragon slept, indigenous tribes
thrived for generations near a native harbor.
Eastern Native Americans, more trusting by nature
than the hostile western tribes, were bilked
in unseemly barter for their land, as the Dutch
West India Company established the island city
of New Amsterdam; a gateway to Henry Hudson's
valley north and to the wild, sparsely settled
frontier west. And Dutch interests in the west
were stronger to the south to the islands
of the Antilles (Aruba, Bonaire, and Curacao).

The Old Mill Creek

The Dutch let their early trading posts
fall to English claims with a royal colony charter
granted and a new name, New York, that honored
England's landed Duke of York, who later sat
on the royal throne and who ruled as England's
second King named James. The French, meanwhile,
were exploring to the north, where Champlain founded
the settlement of French Quebec near the lake
that bears his name; its shores outlined by Canada
to its north, and New York and Vermont to its west
and east. True to a previous pattern, French clerics
driven by Richelieu, with hands of ambition stained red
as his cardinal's robe, followed the routes of fur traders
along rivers like the St. Lawrence and posted forts
farther inland by North America's Great Lakes
to the demise of the northeast's Native Americans—
the Iroquois, the Kickapoo, and Huron to name a few.
England, not to be outdone, through royal charters
and joint-stock companies mapped out the east coast
of North America with British colonies that stretched
from New England to the north and the Carolinas
to the south. The British put a collar on their mug
of brew, colonizing the island of Bermuda,
an orphan child, whose sighs of resistance to adoption
and distaste of the burden of restraint from a parent's
overbearing oversight simply went unheeded.
The Bahamas and West Indies, with white sand
beaches of an island chain that dot the royal-blue
waters of the Caribbean, were soon to follow
while the stars that dominate the sky at night
looked down helplessly upon their own reflections
cast on the canvas of a glass-topped, calm flat sea.
From Jamestown, Virginia, on in North America,
England did not in naked truth have the means,
nor did it at first glance see similar commercial
gain, to replicate the stranglehold it held on India.

Circumstances give rise to opportunity, and cash
crops for the Exchequer's treasury counting room,
first from Virginia tobacco ripe for smoking pipes
and later from Carolina cotton for mills producing
bolts of cloth, spurred English ambition for expansion
in North America with its climate quite tolerable
for waves of British, Scotch, and Irish immigrants,
a sea born migrant caravan to Great Britain's
New World colonies. But disputes and civil war
among Anglicans, Catholics, and royalists, against
Puritans and Parliamentarians backed by Scotland
as an early ally in the waging of a British civil war,
spread discord and disruption across the realm.
Not all warring paths lead to a lasting peace
and Cromwell, in parliament's easy victory, roused
Scottish ire purging Presbyterians from its roles.
So short the rest of peace, besieged in discrimination's
shroud, the Scots repulsed, rebelled from Cromwell,
who in another victory's blushing swell, and desiring
further resistance to be quelled, conceded
to a settlement that did not like poor Charles,
cost a king his head; except for some unfortunates
like the Lord of Monmouth and his close associates
whose failed rebellion in 1685 were dispatched
on an English chopping block, and a thousand others
were ordered to be transported to English colonies,
or stay to face the hooded executioner's falling axe.
This was the fate of one such man from a family
of the fifteenth-century Malcom clan from lands
within Scotland's Argyllshire. "Old John"
was born in 1657, and for his suspected sympathies
with Monmouth's failed war with Parliament
was chained with others, more than hundreds
in numbers, shoved into a dank and dirty prison vault
with a single small window that opened to day's
dim light and the brackish smell of the salted sea,

where they languished through the summer's
heat standing in filth and mire an ankle deep.
Finally liberated on conditions of banishment
that was irrevocable, John McCollum, with others
who survived their inhumane imprisonment,
was transported on the ship the *Henry* and *Francis*
to the colony of New Jersey; a journey of many weeks
with sickness and death an unwelcome attendant
for the dozens who death claimed with burial rites
at sea, never to see the landing port of Perth Amoy,
to tread on land near Barnagat, and later settle
near an ancient oak of three-hundred aged-years
in Basking Ridge. It's there where "Old John,"
after a life that spanned a century plus three,
died peacefully at age 103. He lies at rest
next to Mary Bern, his wife, in Basking Ridge
Presbyterian cemetery just beneath a new church
building's sanctuary, as Mary, New Jersey born
in 1676, died as did John, in April 1760.
Mary's and John's head stones still call out
to parishioners and other visitors who stop by
and pause to read their weathered headstones.
Their markers are placed alongside the rebuilt
church not far from the shadows of the shade
that once prevailed from an ancient oak that lived
for six-hundred years before it gave up its ghost—
so went the soul of the city of Basking Ridge.
John, the older of the two, warns passerbys
to be ready when death, soon or long delayed
comes with a king's warrant that is irrevocable:
You Old and Young, you Middle Aged, Great & Small.
Take my advice; be ready for Death's Call.
I once was Young and many Days did See;
I Dy'd when Old no Age from Death being free.
I'm now Twom'd; in Earth's Dark Cavern Lye
Conquered by Death, Made Ready All in Dye.

And Mary's headstone, she a mere child
with 84 birthdays tolled, provoked an urgent
caution to the women of her time:
You females all, you virgins fair, behold;
Your time's more precious than ye Mass'y Gold.
Your glass runs fast, ye days hurl to an end.
Death will arrest you er'e you apprehend.
Warning ye take, prepare fast for ye grave,
from which no age, no mortal can ye save.
Meanwhile, other families made the way
across the sea in ships that transported immigrants.
Quakers first, then others seeking religious freedom
like Presbyterians who this time came voluntarily,
heeding William Penn's call to sail the sea
to Philadelphia, and settle in along his colony's
southern border, a Protestant bastion to impede
an undesired religious incursion from Catholics
living near the northern edge of Lord Baltimore's
royal Catholic colony of Maryland.
So it was that the Kyle family, descendants
of one Patrick born in 1600 in Ayrshire, Scotland,
and buried seventy years after in the north
of Ireland, made their way to Philadelphia
in the early decades of 1700 when grandson,
James Kyle and Susan Dickinson, his wife,
migrated to the south and west to Lancaster,
and are buried in unmarked graves in Donegal's
Presbyterian Cemetery, in the borough of Mount Joy.
On separate journeys west from the colonies
of New Jersey and Pennsylvania to Connecticut's
Western Reserve in the Ohio wilderness went
Joshua Kyle, Patrick's great grandson times four,
and Mary Stewart, his wife born in Londonderry;
and, too, John McCollum, whose father David,
was the son of "Old John" and Jane Ayers,
the elder John's wife, a child of an early prominent

family from New Jersey's Basking Ridge.
To travel west was not an easy task, as pioneers
came intrepidly by foot and horse-drawn wagons,
their footsteps echoing from a distant time
with wagon wheels encountering rough-cut roads
and trails, mired in muddy pools or assaulted
by sun baked hardened ruts, that now are covered
with the paved concrete and black asphalt
of Interstate 76 on its winding way west
over the top of the Allegheny mountain range;
later home to Grant's and Lee's trails
to blood-soaked battlefields of another civil war,
a fool's game of strategy played out on the hallowed
battle grounds of Gettysburg, where brothers
on both sides, like heaven's warring angels, died.
Such a sad replay of the great-winged brothers
Michael and Lucifer, hornless centurions
of God most high, and their legions battling
savagely to oblivion's dread end, waged within
God's golden gates—the universal crease in eternity
that mortal men in songs with pleadings sing
to their deities in hopes for everlasting openings.
John Forbes, a British General, is credited for a path
he cut in 1758; a route that he with British troops
in tow used in their march over the Alleghanies
to lower land where mountains accede to hills
in Westmorland county close to the confluence
of three rivers giving way, converged in to one.
Traveler's accounts of the journey west
do not sharply criticize the long miles logged
from Penn's Philadelphia to Shippensburg,
but most lament the stark hardships and difficulties
they found along the way, marked by 150 miles
of inhospitable, charmless challenges
through Carlisle, Sidling Hill, on past Somerset,
with no relief from nature's stubbornness until

they reached the sanctuary city of Pittsburgh.
This stop marked William Penn's last grasp
before pioneer settlers made their way west
into the virgin wilderness of the Ohio territory,
seeking land surveyed in metes and bounds
for purchasers desiring plotted deeds outlined
in the mapped details of the Western Reserve;
the Ohio territory's pristine preserve for colonial
Connecticut to parcel out to adventurous travelers,
whose souls undaunted, bravely or foolishly
much the same, set out upon an uncertain journey,
step by arduous step they came, some stopped
and settled along the way of the 500 hundred-mile
trek from the faraway shores of the eastern
colonies to the promised lands of embellished
possibilities in the outskirts of the Ohio territory.
Westmorland was, for many a settling place,
but for some families who had children
and grandchildren born in the east coast's
British colonies, there was land available
in generous tracts for venturous souls
to purchase west of Pittsburgh, Pennsylvania.
Words of the Dauphin Prince fit these hardy folk
like a tight-fit coat, and unlike Louis who spoke
a sad refrain for the loss at sea of reinforcements
for advantage in France's war with England,
the pioneers chose to seek out the favorable
adventures of newborn days in a spirit of buoyed
optimism that urged them on to what in our time
became known, to you and I, as the resplendent
park of Youngstown, Ohio's Old Mill Creek.
Joshua and John made their separate ways
to purchase land within Connecticut's claim
to the Ohio territory, others in their family lines
stayed behind in Jersey or in Lancaster County's
farm rich land; while other relatives trekked South

among the Scotch and Irish immigrants who traveled
past the mountains of Virginia singing songs
with a folksy flavor bolstered by the quickened
pace of background sounds that poured out
from wood carved flutes and jumped from fiddles
guided through their ancient scores by nimble
fingers across taunt strings set to burst on fire.
John and Joshua, both veterans of the War of 1812,
John with Colonel Rayen and Joshua with General
Harrison, found their Ithaca in large tracks
of family farms in Canfield and Austintown
and along the waters of the Axe Factory Run
and Old Mill Creek which snaked a course down
from Alliance to Austintown, on to Youngstown
and the river of the mills that grew like wild
mushrooms, and later smelt iron ore and steel rolls
and ingots that defined a valley that bore its name,
the Mahoning, which white men's legends
claim is an Indian name meaning "at the licks."
No one knows for sure how John's son, Ira,
met Joshua's daughter, Hannah, and how love
proceeded among the two; perhaps these two
met before they married on trips like the one
of April 9, 1834, when Ira hauled a load
of boards in a horse-drawn wagon for one
dollar and fifty cents to his future father-in-law's
timber mill, an early pioneer entrepreneurial
enterprise that now lies under Glacier Lake.
Now, the course of love that flowed
through Hannah Kyle and Ira McCollum
will forever be left for speculation's guessing
game, but this is as certain as night gives way
to the dawning day, from these two came
the union that later gave life's birthing gift
to the writer of this tale of a western trail
that lead my ancestors to the Old Mill Creek.

We have reached the end of the tale of how
two families came to one, and how amidst
the chaos and the randomness of our universe,
ancestors met and like a billion atoms moving
frantically, colliding rampantly creating endless
possibilities, I became the one that is the one
and only one that is me; unique within
the fermenting cosmos of a pulsing eternity.
One last thing before I leave to write other poems
that demand their time to escape the tangles
in my mind, and propelled by the creative surge
that moves all things, strive in audacious optimism
for a temporary reprieve from the swirling chaos
of the elliptical spiral of our universe of uncertainty.
I must, as you, in humble gratitude say "thank you"
to Volney Rodgers, a conservationist like Theodore
Roosevelt but on a smaller scale, both of whom
preserved for posterity our country's natural
parks and nature's bequest to our planet earth's
green and blue treasured jewels which provide
the food that we consume, the air we breathe
to fill our lungs with oxygen, and clean fresh water
that, if managed well, will satisfy the thirst of all
the sacred living things that grace our earth,
and also stir inspiration's magic bubbling pot
for our souls' nourishment so, we, humankind,
might be blessed to find our peace and sustaining
bliss in thoughtful contemplation and meditation
in that elusive awakened state of pure stillness
and the joy of a faithful servant of the enigma
of the Tao, whose muted secrets we can only see
the edges of, as human labels, however craftily
thought out, are inadequate for the task of naming
the unnamed One, and satisfactorily unravel
the inscrutable mystery of how fullness comes
only to those who consciously pursue the transient

state, the venerated place of mindful emptiness.
In the end emptiness, the mind of no mind,
is the route I believe we must trust to journey upon
if we are to experience the fullness of this life;
for you must first close your eyes before you
can open them to see the shadows faintly
outlined, hidden within the shade of night.
Our journeys cannot be measured or metered
out on a line of time that poet's rhyme
with some defined beginning and a certain end;
for they, as we, are but a swirling, whirling circle
game that finds expression in a sacred moment's
flicking within life's deathless burning flame.

The Old Home Cemetery

A white post fence nestles close,
adjacent to the edge of a natural
deciduous forest, centuries old.
Within its fold, row upon row
of weathered headstones unfold.
I slowly open the cemetery gate
and enter tentatively within.
My eyes are drawn momentarily
to a thick, surrounding forest canopy
and gaze upon the stately sentinels
that stand and shade the holy ground.
These proud sentinels—green-capped
in summer time, gave off life-sustaining air,
which along with nature's gift of rain
sustained their once-living charges.
The stoic trees bore silent watch
and witness for decades passing by;
until, some after a century of labor's
unflagging duty were unceremoniously
discharged, recalled, and fell, crashing
silently to the forest's verdant floor,
where they now lay while others grow
to take their post along the forest's edge.
Step after step, I pass by a stone marking
out a place of rest beneath my feet.
The marker calls out to me that someone
who once walked above the ground,
now lies in rest within the earth's embrace;

held tight as a mother snugs a child
close to her soft consoling breasts.
They are there now; the markers
tell me so. I pause while my mind
considers in its own unhurried time
how best to frame and then to ask
the questions that no grave marker
alone can ever satisfactorily answer.
Are you there? If not, where?
And where pray tell were you and I
before we walked upon this earth?
And what of the planets, the night stars
and galaxies eons come and gone?
Where? Do they not reside somewhere
beyond the awareness of my mind?
The answer is not easily obtained,
but it's impermanence that seems
to reign supreme in our realities.
I sit on a white wooden bench,
and like earth renewed by a steady
summer rain, I absorb the sight,
the sounds, the scents in the air
of the old family Home Cemetery.
It is a place of rest for generation
after generation of my father's
hardy pioneer family. Row upon row
of markers call out their names
and shout out, to all who chance
to happen by: "I, too, once lived,
and breathed, like you, and walked
above this ground that is now my home."
As I gaze out, I know deep within
my soul that stars were born to die;
the case for everyone, including me.
Day does give way to night, eternally.
But, is it not equally so that night too

gives way to day, sunset to sunrise?
Light dawns, life emerges, and the cycle
churns and turns without escape—in rhythm
with life's coquettish universal flux.

The Caretaker

Hour by hour, he walks a line
undefined by relentless time.
He counts the posts between
the white fence, ten-foot rails
that mark the way along a border
where visitors may come and go
without the passport residents
surrender when night arrives
and they, with thoughts left behind,
must stop and stay.
Once around the gated fence
the old caretaker sets a guardian's pace
to walk unseen and check each residence
within the charge of his watchful eyes.
He'll often pause to gaze at an entry door
and try to recall each inhabitant
who purchased ground and settled in.
It's true that many came late,
long after the land they bought
through an agent closed.
But a few, he remembers, came
in haste, rushed to settle in; their doors
too soon to shut upon a setting sun
giving way to an early morning frost.
He remembers young Tom Kyle
who in 1824 was first to arrive.
At the age of 21, a time when a family
strived mightily not to abandon all hope,

as Tom fell from the roof of the barn
he helped his father build; the barn
across the street from the old homestead,
the barn that later burned in flames,
in a blazing hearth, down to ashes
and to the soot that lay upon
its charred foundation stones.
Young Tom's residence was but
one hundred yards or so from
the barn from which he fell, and
and little more than twice as far
from the pioneer homestead his father
and mother, Joshua and Mary, started in 1798.
Others came in their due time
taking leave of the old homestead,
but little Billy came when pneumonia
called at age eight, in 1933, and his brother
Steward cried when he and his siblings,
hidden behind a curtain drawn,
while Billy lay in the parlor room
transfixed in wait for his final trip across
the street to night's long residence, heard
their mother say, as cruel as death can be,
"If someone had to leave our house so early,
why not Stewie with his clubbed foot?"
The caretaker's eyes would always tear
when he walked by Billy's place
and recalled Stewie's painful suffering;
a wound that spanned a lifetime,
a tortured path of remorse and guilt
that in his wounded silence was not betrayed,
and pierced Stewie's heart, his spirit
and soul to their fragile fractured core.
For 50 years and more the watchman
made his rounds, before another child
whose promises cut short did not endure,

as she laid early claim to her residential lot.
Erin, linked with Young Tom's parent's
family line could not benefit from modern
drugs, medical miracles that would
have canceled Billy's early closing time.
And the vile devil-beast, the cancer plague,
the scourge that takes precious things,
kin to Shakespeare's *Tempest* epilogue,
a vanquished mercy undelivered from
a chorus of angels urgent prayers
claimed Erin's youthful passport
at the open gates of the white-railed fence.
The watchman saw a short stout man
come every day for years on end
sit on the white wooden bench within,
while mortal fate contentment failed
and his hair from grey to white unveiled
in his melancholy visits to Erin's place;
a sanctuary where summer roses grow
and a dolphin statue leaps and flies
to escape its sea-bound home momentarily.
Every day and every night since 1824,
the loyal caretaker, his charge's liege,
made his rounds, duty bound to walk
and watch while others in silence slept.
He is the kindly phantom wanderer
who came to love so many he never
knew with love in life's embrace.
He is the loyal sentinel who keeps
the crows that roost in day on treetop
limbs from spooking daytime visitors,
and waves away the bats in nighttime flight
from swooping down to cling and hang
on decorated residential entry doors.
Still today, two centuries past, the shadow
man, who kept his watch with loving sight

and care, is in truth the kindly Ghost
of the old Home Cemetery; the other-world
trusted guide from the revenant, the faithful
servant of all who wish to visit with the spirits
who in nature's timeless peace reside.

Magic in the Trees

"It speaks to the all the trees.
Can you hear the woodland's
trees when they speak to me?
It's magic, don't you see?
If you are still and very quiet,
you, too, can hear the forest trees
speak softly, quietly to you,"
I said to my children, while
we stood in the midst of a lush,
venerable old forest, a thousand-years
of trees, one after one, up
from the damp forest floor,
tree after tree, for much of our mother
earth's more recent lease of the grand
expanse we have labeled eternity.
"Who father," my son and daughter
quizzically put the question to me.
"Why the forest trees of course;
they commune with the Wantanabi,
the tree-talker spirit guide, and through
it they can speak with you and me.
They hear and sense, they feel
the coming of the rushing wind
that breaks the stillness in the air.
In that way, they are quite similar
to you and me, and other living things.
The trees are no different from us walking
on their fertile base, feeling the rain

that touches their leaves or needles
as the case may be, and that falls
upon the ground below to wet
the soil that adds the earthen mud
accumulating on our walking shoes
as we proceed to stroll along an old dirt
trail, while the mist in an early morning
fall, lifts slowly from the Lily Pond
and vanishes phantom-like into
the forest's dense, towering canopy."
I tell my daughter and my son,
"Stoop down, grab a handful of forest
soil in your palms, lift it to your nose
and smell the loom, the precious ground
that nourishes all these trees, as it does
for you and me and all the other animals
who are fortunate to share the earth with us.
We are one, you and I, all of nature,
all alive in this magic woodland of trees."
"But, dad," my daughter asks,
"how can that gnarly stick you named
the Wantanabi tree-talker, spirit-rod,
speak with trees and through it the trees
in turn can speak with you and me?"
"To us, sweetheart," I said gently.
"We must not forget your brother
whose eyes with wonder look
at the tallest of the trees
that form along the path above
the course of the Old Mill Creek."
"The squirrels, rabbits and raccoons,
the fox and skunk and deer,
they can hear the trees, they, too,
can hear the sounds they speak."
"I think the magic lay quietly
upon the forest floor, waiting patiently

for someone coming by, someone
like you, who could see its possibilities
to open up a dialogue with the trees, plants
and animals of this woodland paradise."
"The gnarly stick, I'm sure was once
a trusted limb on an old wise, wizard tree.
You picked it up and set it free.
We took it home and welcomed it.
Your brother and I cleaned off
the coated mud attached to it,
and we three, like indigenous people
have for hundreds of centuries past,
painted colorful symbols on the stick;
breathed life, resurrected, and renewed
the Wantanabi staff so long asleep,
as a newly fashioned walking stick—
our own small, symbolic totem pole."
"It's alive," I said gleefully!
"Soon, kids, we will take it with us
and walk again along the earthen trail.
We will tap the stick against what look
to be the oldest ones among the trees,
and try to talk with the cautious spirits
of our new, mystical woodland friends."
"Then we'll hike up the two-hundred-foot hill
from the Lily Pond and enter into
the old Home Cemetery, a safe sanctuary,
a small city where mother earth holds within
its loving arms your great-grandparents
and their mothers and fathers, too;
all resting peacefully now generations past,
these immigrants from colonial times,
Scotch-Irish protestants that immigrated
from Argyllshire and Londonberry."
"Oh, dad," they both protested;
"must we go to such a scary place?"

"Don't worry," I replied, "cemeteries are not
the frightening places Halloween portrays
or horror movies terrorize on a movie screen.
They are quiet, intimate, restful places
where kind old spirits sometimes abide,
like the regal trees we stop to see
and chat with, if they're so inclined."
"Besides, you'll be with mom and me,
if we can persuade her to come with us,
and we will have the Wantanabi;
our tree-talking spirit stick, to breach
the quietness we perceive within the air,
if there are friendly spirits hanging out
who in a new encountered trust decide
to discard their customary silent code in favor
of communication and have a friendly chat with us."
I paused to let the information settle
in and then said to my children,
"We will walk down the road
past our pioneer family's old stone
homestead, built before Ohio was a state,
and then walk back into the park."
"We'll look down, beyond West Glacier
Drive, upon the lake that long ago
was a natural march before a dam
was built that trapped the water
flowing from the Axe Factory Run
and Mill Creek, sibling tributaries
to each other and to the larger river
that gave its name to the Mahoning
Valley; a place where mills popped up
like mushrooms along its banks
and smelt sheets and tubes of steel
from melted iron ore in giant fire
furnaces that spewed black sulfur clouds
of smoke into Youngstown's soiled air."

I mentioned that their great grandfather,
who's grave we walked by, worked
in a mill for forty years until one day,
Black Monday it was called; a day
of infamy when tens of thousands
of seasoned steel workers shed
a million tears in disbelief as factory gates
were closed, furnaces grew cold,
and mills were abandoned, shuttered
to rust and rot in toxic brown fields
like dinosaurs lost to a hundred years
of winter-night that cruelly came
in the fallout from a meteor's crash
and life imperiling, fiery burst of deadly
searing heat and blinding light."
"Just like that," I continued, "the river lost
U.S. Steel, Bethlehem, Republic and
Youngstown's homegrown Sheet and Tube."
All this chaos occurred, I explained,
despite the shift long ago from pig iron
pipes to manufactured rolled sheets of steel.
I did not hesitate to tell the hard truth
that this was the same Sheet and Tube
caught up in 1916 and 1937 fights
for worker's rights and benefits,
and union representation to bargain
for a fair measure of laboring men's
contributions to the profits flowing
to the owners of unregulated, greedy,
monolithic business enterprises.
"And sadder than a fallen angel's doleful
lament," I proclaimed to them, "violence,
as dangerous as a serpent's raised head,
erupted in an angry molten lava flow,
when hired mercenaries and complicit
local police were bought with management's

deep pockets, flush, full of cash to pay out
bounties to agents of containment and control."
We talked about the bloody aftermath,
where injured workers locally and 400 miles
to the north and west, near a Great Lake's shore,
were cast as thugs and criminals, while some paid
the highest price and lost their life in the noble
fight for worker's rights to a living wage
and calling for a safe workplace.
I was focused on our son, who at nine
was fascinated with a butterfly
that had landed softly on a forest twig,
while our daughter who was thirteen
asked me pointedly why the owners
of the mills could not find a compromise
that advanced a common good with the workers
who labored in their factories. I just paused,
and answered truthfully that lack of empathy
and unbridled greed was reason's deadly enemy.
Our son looked up and said to me with enchanting
precocious innocence, "Why not ask the trees?"
My son and I stood by while our daughter
took the Wantanabi walking stick, tapped
along a side of the wide circumference
of a large, old elm tree nearby, and waited
for the tree to share with us its secrets
of the forest's way to live in peace among
the many trees who seemed to thrive in harmony.
I waited carefully to hear the tree speak back
to me, when my children asked if the trees
had spoken words to me. I said, with genuine
sincerity, "The forest is filled with empathy
and cares for all the precious living things
that grace the forest from its fertile floor
up to its highest canopy that reaches out
to see the clouds, absorb the rain

and feel the warming sun. Its secret
is that the trees care so much for us,
they take in our lung's carbon waste
and unselfishly give back to us pure
oxygen-rich air for our lung's to taste,
to savor, and to freely breathe."
We took a few deep breaths and passed
the Wantanabi stick from hand to hand,
and then the three of us, arm in arm retraced
our path back along the Old Mill Creek trail.
Once safely home, we placed our beloved
Wantanabi spirit guide sentimentally within
its favored place inside, in a tall wicker
basket nestled near our home's front door.
Then I said to my family, "Next week
we will hike to Bear's Den, a place
of giant rocks and caves, where Indian
legend says bears once denned."
My wife declared that a mother should
come along on such a trip, and the children
and I all lit up with excitement we could
not contain; and then, as a family, we agreed
that we would search the rocks and caves
for ancient drawings painted long before
the Indians came; a time of myth and fantasy,
a time, I fancied, when great winged dragons
were said to hide in wait within the Bear's Den
caves to drag unsuspecting intruders deep inside.

The Dragon's Lair

The Wantanabi waited patiently,
standing silently on its faithful watch
for the sure and certain coming
of a cheerful morning sun.
The Wantanabi has an optimistic soul.
Forget the image of a crooked walking
stick held by an old, nasty, wrinkled troll.
The wooden Wantanabi shames the hopeful
souls of focused men, vigilant and poised
to snatch a revelation moving in the clouds,
night's guiding stars, the season's change,
the harvest and the hunt, the sound of flowing
water; the promise of a homecoming to Eden's
banished garden; a point on a half-formed map
to Europe's west, where trees of life abound
and the flaming swords of warrior angels
are not brandished to block the way
to the paradise centered on a grist mill creek's
flowing watercourse, passing by a group of caves
where an ancient breed of bears once denned.
In my dreams, I have heard a troubled loon
sing a song of mourning from nature's reverie,
a dirge of dire prophecies that I cast aside,
"Too soon," I say cautiously, for I will not
concede that we are cursed and doomed.
I sense deep within my inner-being
that we are linked along a circular path
with guiderails as a cautionary chaperone;

connected with the spirits of pious devotees
whose mystical souls vibrate in harmony
with nature; driven by a quiet contemplative
mind and the daily, faithful practice of ancient
rituals of arms and legs that flow effortlessly
in fundamental moves and forms in the once
secret Katas of the temple monks.
This is my Wantanabi, the one that adopted
me. Encased within its wooden core, preserved
inside the Hara of my Wantanabi walking stick,
rests a cache of energy that only human hands
can grasp, take hold, and on sensory-laden walks
within the ecological gem of the Old Mill Creek
release the magic held inside its sleeping grain.
I feel the heat of a peaceful glow within
the wizardly wooden stick; in bliss I walk
in harmony with its soul and in a burst of joy
I can breach the forest reverie; shouting out,
in exaltation, a reverberating, echoing Kiai.
Our family council asked collectively,
"Who should hold it first," and three of us
in unison declared that Mom must,
within her gentle, caring hands,
be the first to hold the Wantanabi stick
and start our day-long trek, our walk
from end to end of the full measure
of the natural wonder my father, reverently,
called, nature's gift, the Old Mill Creek.
The hike was one from west to east, a fact
our children observed would mean the sun
would travel opposite and set where we began.
They looked at us, the parents who protected
them and said, "It will be dark by then, and how
is it that you will we get us safely home?"
"Don't worry kids," I replied, "when our
adventure is complete, grandpa will be waiting

in his car at a prearranged pickup point
he and I have previously identified."
We parked our car as near we could
to the Mill Creek's inlet to Newport Lake's
wetlands reserve, and took an uneven earthen
trail that followed the shifting shoreline
of the once largest of three man-made lakes
that trapped the Mill Creek's meandering
water in its flow to its muddy bigger sister,
the sullied, long-defiled Mahoning River.
Eggs and toast our breakfast made,
backpacks filled with healthy snacks
and water bottles slid inside, with shorts
and hiking shoes we set off on our journey;
a nature walk that would take twelve thousand
steps and more before we met my father
for the rescue ride back to our parked car.
"We have the day set aside for family
time," I said earnestly, "to walk together,
to stop and watch and listen in silent
reticence for the forest and its woodland
creatures to speak with us and share,
if the forest spirits deem it so, secrets
of its mysteries, born millennia before."
The children simply nodded heads and asked
with well-founded premonition for assurances
that we planned to stop frequently to rest
and have a snack. My wife cast a surreptitious
look my way as if to say, "Just relax, enjoy
this unfolding day with a minimum of philosophy,
and when you must, keep it bright and light,
free of the darker clouds you often sight."
I shrugged my shoulders and raised my
eyebrows in reply as if to say "understood"
and said, "Let's start our hike of the Old
Mill Creek." The children suggested,

with a question tucked within, their mother
should hold the Wantanabi spirit talking stick
until we took a break and the painted wooden
spirit guide (what to passing eyes was just a gnarly,
twisted walking stick with children's finger-painted
signs and a crook three hands down below its top)
would then be entrusted to another pair of guardians'
hands to carry it farther down the path following
the map our family drew, with stops and points
of interest along the way we all agreed we had
to see. We set down our destination points
purposefully on white typing-paper, using
colored crayons we each selected randomly;
our personal choice to mark an important place.
We were early on our way and our children,
daughter and son, stayed several paces ahead
and were first to see the island of the daffodils
spread across the jut of land off the mainland's
shore. The tiny island resembled the work
of a lava flow from the ocean floor giving birth
to islands in the seas eons of times before
Newport was a lake within the carved-out
gorge of the Old Mill Creek.
"The island is so beautiful, like paintings
from a show hanging on the Butler's walls,"
our daughter said happily. We stopped,
sat down on a fallen tree's still intact trunk
to eat an apple and a slice of cheese, when
our son asked how it was that flowers grew
so abundantly on a scrap of land with water
all around. "Perhaps nature is to the flowers
on that tiny island," my wife responded
gently to our son, "as kind and loving parents
are to the children, like you, who bless
their lives with joy each awakened day."
"Your mother is on to something we should

keep within our consciousness," I exclaimed.
"Did the tree we sit upon speak to share
its wisdom with you through the Wantanabi
stick," I asked my wife deliberately, as we
gazed at each other silently before she said,
"Why, of course, it is our tree-talking spirit guide;
our treasured friend that helps us see, and hear,
and smell what others passing by do not know
the forest freely gives to those who pause
to breathe its fresh and pure unspoiled air."
Once past the dam that formed Newport
Lake, the Old Mill Creek reclaimed
its featured role and the bumpy trail wound
on to follow the creek on a gentle slope,
banking down toward a deeper gorge
of carved out rock in a temperate rush
toward the dam above Lanterman's Falls,
alongside the grist mill built on a ledge
of stone long before Frank Lloyd Wright
drew his plans for Falling Water, a Pittsburgh
titan merchant's summer home designed
by Wright for creation's eyes not to recognize
human intrusion into nature's masterwork.
We climbed the trail which now inclined
toward the concrete roadway bridge spanning
the gorge and creek below, and offered up
a grand view of the falls that cascaded fifteen
feet down past a jutting ledge of stone,
to a deeper pool of water, a pooling place
the forest spirits seemed intent to keep in check
to a quiet, reposed hush when our son asked,
"Can we climb down to the Indian's Ledge to look
for arrowheads that might be found on the ground?
Dad, there might be a few undiscovered, left behind
on that jutting stone ridge; maybe some fell
from a puncture hole in a dangling quiver looped

over the shoulder of an Indian warrior who watched
on guard for intruders from another tribe."
Forgetting my wife's exhortation for a moment,
I interjected, "Or white settlers who abandoned
The Book of Common Prayer they held dear,
and with covetous eyes, bloodied with the madness
that in all of nature afflicts our species most,
looked upon Indian land as an estate to be had."
"You could be right, son," as I reclaimed a level
plane, "perhaps there are a few left behind
from a time when Indians from native tribes
on a sentry's watch would surely have perched
themselves on the cleft of rock above the creek,
and the pointed heads of hard chiseled rock
could have fallen silently, like a leaf freed
to float on a gentle breeze until it landed softly
on the moss that gathers on the smooth rocks
and ragged stones that line the moist course
of a stream born when time itself was so old
its protracted mind turned to forgetfulness."
Our daughter interjected, "If an arrowhead fell
three hundred years ago, do you truly think
it would be lying, undetected on that jutting ledge?"
My wife smiled and replied, "Who can say
with any degree of certainty." Then I added,
"Well, it might have happened long before
this bridge, spanning the gorge, we are standing on,
was a community project calling out 'build me.'"
The weight upon my heart was heavy,
my soul laden without rest, burdened
with Hamlet's guilt, as I looked down
and tried to imagine what centuries past
was a pristine creek with nature's running water
pure and clear, unblemished, safe for all creation's
living things to wade in and to drink.
My wife looked quizzically at me, as if to say,

"Cut your rhetoric down to children's length,"
and apparently concerned with my blitz-like rush
of enthusiasm, "But aren't you quite uncomfortable
with heights, a ladder's steps, not to mention,
if I might, the edge of ledges we have seen
on the trails we've trudged along today?"
I was relieved she chose her words judiciously
and did not embarrass me with the truth that fear
of heights and falling from a ledge was a phobia
that clung to me from nightmares birthed in childhood.
The truth was quite irrefutable. I could not find
a shovel adequate for a laborer's job to dig a hole
deep enough, to entomb within the earth's hard
ground sane irrationality, far from consciousness,
that I might be freed of a primordial dread
that plagues humans readily but does not appear
to cripple other animals with indecision's
hesitancy at stark precipices, that I, trapped
within my phobia, find terrifying and unnerving.
Our daughter, in a spirit of playfulness,
said to her younger brother, "You are more
likely going to find a gang of trolls hiding
under this bridge than Indian arrowheads
from centuries ago." I joined the jousting
tease, "That's right son, remember the passages
within *The Hobbit* book that we read last week?
Well, the Wantanabi just said to me that the trees
are whispering about a time within the gorge
of the Old Mill Creek, like that of Tolkien's
Middle Earth, when fierce dragons were alive;
reptile kings who ruled the sky and land below."
My wife with a sympathetic heart interceded
and interrupted a tease that had lapsed good
humor's tolerance, "Enough of scary, imaginary
stories of nasty trolls and fearsome beasts."
"Oh, sweetheart," I respond to my son,

"your sister and I were merely teasing. We're
sorry if we freighted you. Besides, who knows
if Tolkien got it right that trolls were nasty things
hiding under bridges waiting to exact a toll,
and if dragons were rapacious beasts or merely
creatures with a heartburn trapped deep inside
their armored shells that heated to the seething
point where fire simply had to be released."
And then, the white cumulus within the partly
cloudy sky above moved leisurely along,
tracking with the breeze within the wind.
The sun appeared momentarily and I swore
I saw a glint of green within the rock
behind the jut of protruding stone,
the spirits of the Old Mill Creek in Orphic
sacredness, christened as Indian Ledge.
Little did I know what that window of the sun
foretold, as we moved on to a bench down
the trail to pause for a snack and water break.
We checked off Lanterman on our freelance map,
and agreed that Idora was just up the road,
not too far away, and we should probably move
to the next point of interest on our unfolding
nature walk; "Our marvelous family bonding trip"
I surely uttered twenty times or more that day.
We walked up the inclining road and crossed
to the other side, climbed up a short sloping
berm of grass and shrubs and trees, until
we reached a chain link fence that surrounded
the once fantastic, urban amusement park
abutting God's grand estate, a counter culture
parallel along with sulfur spewing smoke stack mills,
to Youngstown's jeweled gift, the Old Mill Creek.
As we peered inside the aging rusting metal fence
our eyes transfixed on the burnt-out remnants
of the Wild Cat, a wooden coaster that enthusiasts

once ranked among America's top ten rides.
We walked along the two parks' small divide
to a point where we found a breach, a short cut
we could use if we dared enter into a forbidden
zone; a landscape I believe Shakespeare would,
in pained refrain, have said was a burdened place
of troubling images and epithets of the cost
of clashing cultures and the weary toll of war.
My wife and daughter, with better sense,
remained outside; our sentries who could
be a buffer if a park ranger happened by
to stop and ask them if they needed help
with directions to some other place within
what most locals, in typical understated ways,
like toes conjoined that have lost creation's
purpose, simply call "Mill Creek Park."
We entered to a clearing that opened up
to a once fun-filled amusement park, a place
of revelry and family merriment, that I
found reminiscent of Europe's tattered
landscape torn asunder from bombs dropped
to rid the world of the vile monster
of the Holocaust and his poisonous lust
for conquest, his maladjusted madness
for a mythic race of blue-eyed, blond, white
supremists who would rule the world
for a thousand years of tyranny extolling all
who had the fictitious looks and fabricated
claims as members of an imaginary Aryan race.
Our eyes were drawn to a concrete shell
with a dangling painted sign that said
"French Fries," to visitors who hungered
for fresh cut fries with skins intact and extra
salt and malt vinegar to spice them up
for a fried food connoisseur's certain pleasure.
As we neared the entrance to the dilapidated

french fry stand, we stopped, our feet locked
in place in mafia concrete blocks, our walk halted
with dread as we saw the rusting old Royal
Crown Cola soda pop cooler and strange graffiti
markings spray-painted on the walls inside
the french fry stand. My son and I, with fear
creeping into my core, stopped while I,
with a laundered interpretation, declared
that the dread-inducing symbols, rendered
in hieroglyphs patterned from an earlier time,
warned the world and all who were not initiated
into a Youngstown gang, "Come no further,
go away; for those who dare to stay
calamity will follow you all your days."
The interlude was short, but I cannot deny
the chill I felt as the soda cooler looked to me
like a tomb robbed, a desecrated sarcophagus,
and the graffiti on the concrete walls spelled
out in gang-induced hieroglyphics Shakespeare's
epitaph that all who move my bones are cursed.
I said to my son, "Let's leave this place, I don't
feel safe." But my son with childlike innocence
declared, "That's silly, Dad," as we proceeded
to peer inside the empty soda cooler and spent
a moment within the decaying french fry stand.
We left, as best I can tell, without a curse
upon our heads more dread then any of life's
ordinary calamities that bedevil all living things.
My wife and daughter greeted us excitedly
as we returned to the breach in the fence
we entered through. My daughter proudly
stated, "Mom and I did well. We did not
mention you. We told the park policeman
in a cruiser passing by we were taking a break
in our hike to our next location—the Suspension
Bridge, and he just nodded, pointed back and said,

'It's on down that way, have fun, enjoy the park.'"
His concerned mother asked our son, "Well tell us,
how was it inside? Were you surprised, frightened?"
"Not me, I wasn't afraid. I wanted to stay longer,
but Dad said the place was creepy and we
had to get back to you." With a sheepish smile,
I replied somewhat timidly, "While we did
walk around and saw the Wild Cat's still intact
the little sibling. We walked for a short while
on the rickety deserted wooden tracks
of the shorter twists and quick ups and downs
that mimicked the thrills of the junior
coaster ride named for jumping jack rabbits."
My wife, with pointed eyes aimed on a taunt bow
set to hurl sharp rebukes to a guilty transgressor,
mouthed a silent bawling-out, "You did what?"
My son, thank you forest spirits, gifted me
a temporary shield against impending harm
when he blurted out, "And then we went
to a large open-sided building that Dad said
was once known as 'the house of cool.'"
"That's right." I quickly said, relieved
for a moment's reprieve from certain execution.
"We walked on Idora's once-revered Ballroom
floor, and could see the ghosts of Tommy Dorsey's
orchestra, Steubenville's climbing crooner
(later a charter member of Sinatra's pack of rats),
and the golden horn of Harry James and his band
shaking the wooden rafters above, a staccato
vibrating, recalling the sound of trumpets
that brought down Jericho's walls."
My son looked at me and said, "What did
you just say? I never saw a ghost, or heard
the music from some old-time orchestra."
"We'll talk later," was my wife's Miranda
warning, awaiting me when I was alone in her

custody. Our daughter asked, "What's next?
Are we off to explore bear's dens?"
"Yes," I replied, "but first we cross Mill Creek
on the ornate, silver Suspension Bridge, built
with local steel in 1895; the bridge on Valley Drive,
that if you saw in Great Britain would be a site
where a princess bride would take her royal
wedding carriage ride to a castle in the countryside
far outside the noise within the belly of the beast
that was known as iconic London city."
"From there we will turn our heads west."
I said, "let's check our map and head back down
to the Y in the road we did not take, when we
climbed the slope that led up here and breached
the fence that your brother and I used foolishly
to enter into the forgotten park's forbidden zone,"
in the hope that I might ease the interrogation
my darling wife was currently mapping out,
with mild malice certainly on her mind.
"Do you remember what I said about Bear's Den,
last time we did our forest walk?" I asked the
children casually. Then doubt crept into my
inner-psyche as I thought within myself, "It's
locked inside my mind, but does it still sit
and resonate with them?" How sad is it,
how hard that names and memories are so
soon left behind to float away like leaves
gently falling down to disintegrate upon
patient mother earth's awaiting ground.
"Come back from wherever you have gone,"
my wife said mercifully to me. I nodded
thankfully and returned presently to embrace
the moment interrupted before I drifted
dangerously into a melancholy difficult to purge.
My daughter added, strategically, I now recall,
"Give the Wantanabi to Dad. He'll need it for

us to witness and interpret the signs he says
are left behind within the ancient caves."
"Thank you, sweetheart, you are right.
I will need our spirit-talking stick to guide
us as we climb the boulder rocks and enter
the small caves that populate the exploration
area that is next, once we cross the bridge
and follow the path of our home drawn map."
"I remember, Dad," our son said eagerly,
"you said we would search for drawings
in the caves that were made long before
Indians were here; a time of dragons
and other things that have vanished
from the planet that was once their home."
"That's right kids," I replied, while
my wife like a practiced mime stood
still, but her message came clear
as the fullest moon late on a cloudless
night, "Please be very careful here."
As we climbed the large boulder rocks
that time's rains had smoothed like pebbles
polished by running water in a stream,
we all agreed how smart we were for wearing
hiking shoes that aided in the dreams
we brought to conquer rocks, that I said,
to bait the children's appetites, were taller
than a Brontosaurus' stretched-out neck
reaching for the greenest leaves atop
a giant Mesozoic-era tree. Despite
the fact that the rocks were not as towering
as Monument Valley's desert buttes, I urged
my agile wife and children, and more myself
I must admit, "Do not look down, keep your eyes
focused on the rock in front, for all good climbers
turn their faces upwards toward the clouds."
Our daughter and our son seemed as thrilled

as Edmund Hillary standing atop Everest,
with his Sherpa guide, while my wife, and I
especially, felt relief that we had avoided calamity;
no one slipped, no one yelled and fell, our bones
remained intact, unbroken and unharmed.
"What about the caves below these rocks?"
our son buoyed by our climbing success
called out. "Sure," our daughter said,
"we can sit inside the shade a cave provides
and have another snack." To which my wife,
fair goddess, high protectionist of our family's
good health and safety replied with eyes on me,
"Let's check them out and see what we can find
hidden within the outer crevasses, but not
too deep inside the caves beneath the rocks."
I heard the emphasis she placed upon "outer
crevasses," her caution was unmistakable.
We walked by every cave in Bear's Den,
and marked it finished on our map; no bear's
claws left behind to find, no spirit writings
we could see that might appease the dampened
expectations of children on an expedition
of discovery. I looked toward my wife
and our intuitions passed telepathically.
"Well kids, don't be disappointed,"
I gently said. "Your Mom just reminded
me that the Hobbit and his gang of dwarfs,
the adventurers we read about last week,
could not decipher the map to the treasure
buried within in the Lonely Mountain, until
the map was exposed to the full moon's light;
only then did they acquire the special sight
that was necessary to unravel its mystery."
"Dad's right," their Mom interjected,
influentially, "there could be secret drawings
on the walls that have been unseen

from the time they were first painted
because moon beams cannot often reach within
to illuminate the spirit signs left behind
from Dragon's times and later when the Indians
arrived and caused the bears to leave these caves
behind to seek safety and refuge in mountain
forests far from the land of the Old Mill Creek."
We made our way to the Lily Pond as my wife
declared, to calm any angst our children had,
"We won't be climbing up the hill, up to your
father's family cemetery. You walked through
it the last time you took a hike within the park."
"That's right, dear. Besides, the Old Home
Cemetery is not on our map of sites to visit
on this trip," I said reassuringly to the kids.
"Well, let's go. Let's walk all around the asphalt
path that circles the Lily Pond," our daughter
quite impatiently said to the three of us.
So, the Lily Pond unfolded to our curious eyes;
a small ecological universe, a microcosm
of species special to this place on earth,
like a burning candle that welcomes visitors
to a sacred, consecrated holy site.
Our children stopped to feed the dappled
coy, some as large as two-feet long,
clustered near the water's edge, while I
pointed out the snapping turtles sunning
on fallen trees within the pond. I received
a cautioned look from my patient wife,
as I described the turtle's necks to be strong
as steel with jaws as lethal as an alligator.
The children shook their heads to say "no,"
and our daughter said to her brother,
"I feel bad for the frightened frogs hiding
out among the floating islands of lily pads."
We left the Lily Pond behind and walked

toward the spot of our last break, a place
my father called Ski Hill where he and his
siblings sled down on winter's fresh snow.
Our daughter, who had been staring at her hands
as she ate, paused and then asked, "Dad, why
do our hands have four fingers and one thumb
and the feet in our shoes have five toes?"
"Well, let's think about that for a minute or two.
Frogs have four webbed feet, two in the front
and two behind. When frogs are first born
they are tadpoles, fish like things, swimming
in water with no need for webbed feet, at birth,
to move around in the pools of water
where their birthing eggs were so causally laid.
Also, they need gills at that time to take in oxygen
before they grow to the frogs, we saw today
perched upon the Lily Pond's water pads.
Now, humans start out as eggs in a pool
of water trapped inside their mother's bodies;
here, near the stomach and close to the point
of the belly button we each have."
"How did they get there, Dad?" our inquisitive
son, in naive curiosity, quizzically inquired.
"Enough of this talk of eggs, and fingers and toes.
Dad can finish this story another time," my wife
interceded, as she conjured up a thousand
avenging angels with taunt golden bows
and a sky full of arrows set to rain down on me.
"Let's talk about what we will see on the next
stop on our guide map," she said with pointed
finality. As the kids trudged ahead, my wife
turned and said to me, "You reap what you sow
when you dig too deep to explain to children
things at the time where surfaces are fine."
"I know," I replied, "I can't seem to restrain
myself. Thanks. For a moment I felt like I was

a cast away piece of dark burnt toast."
Next up was Glacier Lake and the long walk
on West Glacier Drive toward the dam
and the point the creek was to a river lost.
We trudged along, weary warriors longing
for a homeland campsite to find relief and rest.
My wife whispered to me, "The kids are tired,
their steps are slow and shuffled and their
eyelids are drooping and heavy. I'm not sure
we can make it to the river's course."
"Sweetheart, we can do it. The dam is just ahead,
around the next curve in the road, and once
we are there few steps remain. We'll have met
our goal, and in the glow of that accomplishment
our muscles and our minds, tired and weary,
will be cleansed and soothed of any doubt
we had in starting out and of the pain we felt
in bones we asked as the holy proverb says,
if they could live to see another day."
Resigned, my forgiving wife, with a silent shrug
of her shoulders, said, "Okay, let's just do this quickly
and without you calling out another ancient proverb."
So, we passed by Glacier dam and the water
cascading down for its last run as the Mill Creek,
before it crossed under the old Mahoning Avenue
bridge to merge within the river underneath.
And to the relief of all, my wife and I as much
as the children we earlier assured, my father
was there waiting patiently for us in his old,
beat up Chevy car which to us looked like a limo
with a chauffeur hired to take us safely home.
Grandpa asked the children, before they drifted
off to sleep, what was their favorite part
of our family hike through the Old Mill Creek.
Our daughter said, "The Lily Pond, for me,"
and our son responded, "Grandpa, Idora Park

was interesting, but I'll go with the Indian
Ledge." I just listened, turned to my wife
as we exchanged smiles, and thought to myself
I wonder if our son, too, saw the glint
of green that I saw, as briefly as a lightening
strike on a stormy night, in the stone tucked
behind the precipice of the Indian Ledge.
The children said goodnight to Grandpa
and my wife and I gave him a thankful hug.
On the ride back to our parked car
the kids soon drifted into sleep,
and once home collapsed into their beds.
My wife unloaded the litter from our backpacks
while I put our home-drawn map safely in a desk drawer
and returned the Wantanabi stick to its station
near our home's front door and said rather archaically,
"Be at rest my trusted friend, bide yourself repose
for the moment, for soon I have another venture
planned that may turn out to be our greatest
adventure; one that I believe could come to me
as a welcome friend with a dare in hand."

The Miracle within the Polished Stone

Planning had been in place for weeks.
My father joked that General Eisenhower
did not spend more time planning World
War II's invasion of Omaha Beach.
As I rechecked the gear in our bags,
I thought to myself good naturedly:
now that came from a Navy man, a sailor
who spent the war on a "crash rescue boat,"
(that's right, he said small boat, not ship)
while stationed on Palmyra Atoll, a speck
of land without a castle inside an ocean moat,
alone in the Pacific, a thousand miles
south of the island chain where Japan
launched a surprise attack and brought
the United States into a war that opened up
a door to doom and barbarity; a plague across
the European continent; a savagery as cruel
as enemies hoisted on pikes by Transylvania's
Impaler; a test of the fundamental essence
of humanity's soul, its righteousness and manhood,
to fight an evil that only could be neutered
through the use of force, despite Corinthians'
words that men overcome evil with good.
I know that it is hard to call a war benevolent,
but in this case, I believe, it blocked man's descent
to the lower rings of hell and thus was justified.
My wife and daughter did not bother us much
with inquiries, as my son told his mother and sister

he was sworn to secrecy to his dad and grandfather.
"Grandpa says the mission is top secret," our son
would say, like a brave patriot standing alone
at a wall, "there is nothing more I can say,"
he cautioned, buoyed by the emergent flow
of pre-juvenile discovery and testosterone.
I handed the bags that were filled with our gear
to my father, who carefully placed them in the trunk
of his car, before he said, "I'm sure tomorrow will
be better, no rain like today, just cloudy and wet,
no bother to beavers or sea grunts like us,
immune to falling water and the salt in sweat."
To this day, I cannot say it was an ill-boding
premonition that was the incitement for a night
of agitated sleep, nor at the time when the blight
of guilt intruded into my restless mind,
as a king's deceitful son, a Duke as I recall,
said to his father king, suspicion is a bitter rind,
the haunting ghost that sees avenging angels
and mad dog-men lurking everywhere
set upon to slay plotters where they hide;
snakes poised with the poison of a viper's venom
with fangs that held in waiting the measure of eternity,
to spread ill-willed contagion through a hapless
victim's limbs in veins that turn to purple dread.
But sleep loitered that evening for me, stopped
by an inside block in dreams that were a tangled
mess and mystery, while my son tossed and turned,
up and down, set to sail on an uncharted sea
of emboldened discovery, and my father, for his part,
slept peacefully, as men of a certain age and maturity
of character seem to outward eyes always calm
before the approach of dark Delphian clouds
and the shroud of impending death that blankets
an endangered earth when foul weather advances
steadily like a ravenous beast of prey.

Morning came wrapped in a shadowy ugly mist,
an impotent deterrence to dampen my young son's
exuberance for the clarion call of discovery—
the intrepid adventure about to unfold
that the gang of three could not resist.
And my wife and daughter, still lingering within
the comfort of their beds, looked out their open
windows quietly rejoicing this was one star
they would not be bound to follow with the band
of three whose souls they thought might sail far
and free. But mother and daughter did not discern
how the common duty of the gang of three
was misinformed, suborned to a higher need
to penetrate, to pinpoint something unforeseen.
Two men and one boy foolishly equipped,
armed with chiseling tools to chip away
at the alluring light they had seen from the glint
of emerald green; a tempter's enticing sheen
of a glistening gem, snugged within the space
behind the jutting stone of the Indian Ledge,
where unknown wickedness loomed
high above the pool below, deep and flush
with the water that rushed and fell from the falls
beside old Lanterman's long stilled mill.
Goodbyes were passed on, as we said
from God's gift of Bengali, "We are coming,"
meaning life is always in a state of becoming,
as hugs were exchanged among the loving.
We did not see our mission dangerous,
nor was it to our complicit minds nefarious.
We did not feel the need for a prayer.
We saw no coming perils, but stealth
and a hunter's cunning were essential
elements of a strategy we set upon,
as we spied with the tools of a lion waiting,
watching patterns of the park police patrols passing

along the streets near and above the Indian Ledge.
To repel down the cliff, and access the cave
behind the ledge, would require time enough
to anchor safety hooks, climber's cams
to hold a man secure, descending down the cliff
to reach the small space behind the ledge.
Once there, we would learn painfully
that emerald eyes of green, long perceived
as nothing more than dead stone with a glint
of green within, revealed a master of deceit,
for the stone still had the faintest residue
of endangered life ensnared within the final
throes of death's dread, consummating rattle.
I thought that I should be the one to drop down,
to place the cams like rungs upon a ladder,
for my father to follow while my son stood guard
for us; our assurance that we would be safe
to do our work unobserved from interfering eyes
that would otherwise alert authorities who would recall
us from, what to them, was untenable, an egregious,
unauthorized trespass in their park; a breach
of etiquette as sour as is written or recorded
in any of misfortune's classic, discomforting books.
But like a prince deferring to the seasoned wisdom
of a respected king, I did not wish to seem a foolish
son who in a rush of self-indulgent enthusiasm
would drag the shadow of calamity to cast grey
shade upon a father's best intentions for his son.
From below the road, just out of sight, we anchored
our climbing rope around the thick trunk of a Douglas
Fir more than thirty feet tall, as my father began
to descend to a crack where he set the first cam
safe in place, held tight in the rock that loomed
well above the outcrop of stone called Indian Ledge.
Another six feet, and a cam set in place,
put my father three feet from the precipice

of Indian Ledge. He looked up as a good
climber should and said, "Next drop, will put me
right on the ledge." While I thought
to myself, we're not far from the floor of the cave
we are certain lurks within, obscured
from the light of our radiant sun and the lessor
luminosity of a shy moon, carved from an earlier
time when the creek's gorge was first formed,
ten-million years after the dinosaurs died,
ten-million years before tribes of Indians arrived.
As my father dropped and swung his legs
toward the under-ledge to gain a foothold
on the damp cliff rock of the mysterious cave
we obsessed to see, I found myself
Prometheus Bound as a tempest fell on me.
I trembled and shook in panic, believing
we had wronged our great mother earth
as a burst of air, a wind shear I was sure,
with the force of a canon repulsed my aging
father from the front of the ledge, a thunderous
force that propelled him to the cliff wall behind,
striking and injuring his skull as blood flowed red
over the crew cut hair on the top of his head.
I cried out to my son to come help me pull
on the rope to hoist up my father who seemed
to be unaware of his precarious dangling state.
My son pulled with the strength of a grown man,
as adrenaline coursed through his small limbs
and hysteria gripped his mind as he shouted out,
"Tell me, Dad, that grandpa is not dead."
Our breath constricted in labor's merciless
demand, I barely could utter a word
to my son, other than "Just pull on the rope
as hard as you can; we need to get grandpa
up to the road to our car as fast as we can
and take him to the hospital for medical help."

Our muscles burned as if they were torn
on a torturer's rack, as we gasped, spent
warriors collapsed with my injured father
bleeding and unconscious by our side.
"I'll run, get the car and be back in a minute.
Meanwhile, untie the rope from the trunk
of the tree and free grandpa from the climber's
harness that's belted around his waist. We can't
leave those behind," I said to my son
as I raced like a sprinter to our parked car
in the Lanterman lot. My son, while he waited
for me to return, had tears in his eyes and blood
on his hands as he talked to his grandfather, alive
but unconscious and unaware of the ride
to the hospital on Youngstown's south side.
In the car on the way, I had to say to my son,
"This is our story, it's simple and plain;
we were walking the trail above Lanterman's Falls
when grandpa slipped on the moss covering
wet rocks and fell back striking his head
on a large rock sticking out on the wet dirt path."
"Are we in trouble, Dad? Are we going to jail?
Will grandpa be okay, or is he going to die?"
my son cried out in agony. "No, everything will
be okay, and grandpa will get well, but we must
never tell anyone the truth about today. That is
why we could not leave the rope and harness
behind and I threw them into the trunk of our car,
far from the curious eyes of those who would
not understand the goodness in our hearts
for the adventure today we planned to share."
"What about the climbing cams," my son asked
excitedly. "Don't worry," I replied, "they are fixed
in fissures and cracks in the rock that no one will see."
As we pulled the car to the Emergency canopy,
I swore at myself: What damned mischief have I

entangled us in; what need for discovery consumed
my mind and took my father, son, and I on a ship
with Odysseus to daunting dangers and life-
threatening risks unknown to the loyal men who
incautiously trusted to accompany their voyager
king into currents and caves and hidden things.
So, our story was set and my son never flinched
when he and I were questioned about the accident.
Grandpa was a slow walker who lagged behind,
and neither my son nor I, could say with certainty,
but he must have slipped on a wet rock and fell backwards
to land hard on the backside of his crew-cut head.
All we heard, before we turned, was as a guttural sound
that pierced the air like the howl of a wolf
snared in a trap whose cry was a rage rushed
on the wind to bite free of death's iron teeth.
The doctors said my father's injury was deep,
a serious wound with an uncertain fate,
and all we could do, like guards on the wait,
was to stand by his bed and watch him sleep.
My wife and my daughter and son were quite
unnerved when the police came again to father's
hospital room to go over details one more time
with my son and I. "A freak and tragic
accident," I said, "my dad will tell you how
unfortunate it was when his tongue, no longer
silent and still, breaches the barriers
of sound short delayed, like the thunder
that comes after the sight of the flash
of a great spark in a troubled sky."
The detective started to write a note in a pad,
but stopped, looked at my wife and just shook
his head, and leaving said, "I hope the old
man comes back to you soon. I'd love
to sit down with him to have a quick chat."
Three days had passed and nothing changed,

which the doctors said was an encouraging sign.
The longer he is stable the better the chances
his injuries will heal was the mantra they repeated
whenever they visited his hospital room
with windows that looked out on the old cemetery
across the street at Oak Hill. Now who builds
a hospital next to a cemetery, filled with creepy
mausoleums and crypts except some kind of ghoul,
I thought to my troubled and confused inner self.
My wife said to me as I sat in a chair near my
father's bed, "Your mood is so melancholy
and burdened with dread. I think it would be best
for the children and I to stay home for a few days,
as I'm afraid they'll otherwise catch your contagion,
and like you fall prey to a darkness that thwarts
dawn's emergent light, in the comfortless cold
of winter's cruel, unforgiving despair." I nodded
approval with little attended thought and said
to my family, "Stay home for a while, and please
watch out for each other like the night birds
that sit on the peak of our house."
Only later did I learn and understand how
deeply disturbed our son was with fear
that the climbing cams left secure in clefs
in the rocks at Indian Ledge would come back
to the intractable suspicions of guilty minds
caught in a web of lies, if the police or some
meddling hiker's eyes caught sight of the signs
of mischief on the rock wall by Lanterman's Falls.
My son told his mother he was riding his bike
to play baseball all day with friends at the Ridge.
And having no hint that mischief was hiding
inside our son's head, as he covered his deception
in his own art of war, my wife was relieved
as she saw him start off on his ride to Rock Ridge.
But as soon as the boy was out of sight,

he veered down the hill as fast as he might
past the road named McCollum into Mill Creek,
where he sped to the spot of the Indian Ledge.
Putting his bike out of sight, like troops in a jungle
covering their gear, he pulled out the rope
he packed in his bag stashed under his ball glove
and cleats, put my work gloves on his hands,
tied the end of the rope secure round his waist,
and looped in his lead through the first cam.
The boy breathed out a sigh, like a hunter
relaxing before pulling a trigger that would
propel a bullet toward its unsuspecting prey.
Then with no affirmation of what he might find
he slowly lowered himself one hook at a time,
beside Indian Ledge close to the spot where
his grandfather encountered some mysterious force
near the cave we speculated was hidden inside
the stone behind that gave off that intriguing,
glistening hint of sparkling emerald green.
Compared to his grandfather, his weight was much
lighter and the arc of his swing much higher,
so, he had no difficulty landing with both feet
on the outcrop of rock tucked underneath.
He grabbed one of the two extra cams he had
with him in case of a need, and tapped it in place
with the small hammer he had looped through
his belt. By the third tap the cam was anchored
in place and he felt safe, only momentarily
for as he exhaled, he heard the deep sound
of a low growling voice, "I saw you with
the old man the other day, and now I see you,
little boy; you and your annoying hammer.
You are disturbing my day. Do you understand,
boy? Just go away from the entrance to my cave."
Our son later said that sound of the voice
chilled him like a raw winter gale assaulting

rigid, exposed, childhood bones.
The boy, not quite nine, turned toward
the low rumbling sound of the menacing
voice deep as the waters that thundered
over the falls of Niagara; the cascading river
that generates mist for the wind to lift up
to the platform where tourists gather to watch,
and all are tested to resist the wild call of the falls
to be pulled to the crest of the surging water,
to plunge over the edge to a certain death
in the reaping whirlpool waiting below.
The voice went silent as a submarine on alert.
The boy was frozen in place with his eyes
straining to see in the dark of the space behind
the outcrop of stone of Indian Ledge.
It's then that he saw a slit high in the wall
one blink revealing an iris
of emerald green with a golden pupil
in the center of an eye that startled the mind
of a boy on a mission to gather and dispose
of the evidence of climbers who foolishly
challenged the park rules of Mill Creek.
Our son later told us at that moment he realized
he had no weapon sufficient to fight a beast
or a spirit, or whatever it was; but fear
did not linger to the extent that he felt
the urgency to take flight from the site
that caused great harm and grievous injury
to an old man that he respected and loved.
The small boy took a step forward, pointed
the penlight he held in his left hand, tightened
the grip of his right hand on the metal handle
of the claw hammer he brought to Indian Ledge
with obvious intent, then raised his right arm
with revenge as an aim, and said to the voice:
"I don't know what you are other than some

evil thing that troubles my dreams, but you
seriously harmed my grandpa and I want to stick
the claws of this hammer deep into what looks
like the eye of a devil beast afraid to come out;
your wickedness exposed in the light of the day."
"Silly little boy, turn out that light, you don't need
to shine it on me to you see that I'm entombed
in the stone of the wall. My hour of death
has been much delayed. I've been dying
for ten-million years, a death as slow as imagined,
as long as the stars that explode and implode
in skies of the night-heavens, so far beyond
the reach of the things that come and go
on this island of blue and green in a turbulent
sea of swirling, colliding galaxies."
"What are you," the boy asked the voice.
"I am, I was once I should say a dragon,
King of Avian. My name is Gregore,
some even called me the one who is great."
"Well you are not great to me. My grandfather
is a great man. He's the man you have hurt.
And how can you lie that you have been dying
for such a long time? How is that possible,"
the boy asked the voice and the eye in the stone.
"Huh," said the voice, "I guess young boys,
two-legged arrogant things, too human since Adam's
precipitous fall, don't known the truth about dragons.
Well, I'm the last of my kind, the one left behind.
I can tell you that dragons die very slowly,
slower than a crawling glacier's pedestrian pace;
an inch a year from a mountain top through
a valley to the sea below is like a thorough-bred
horse sprinting on a race track, when compared
to the rate of a wounded dragon's passage from life."
"You're a dragon," the boy responded incredulously.
The irritated voice shot back, "Look in the stone,

not at my eyes. A closed mind with open eyes
will never see beneath the thin veneer of a dark
night that tries to hide and obscure
the hard truths and tenants of uncaring reality."
The boy, for a moment, let his mind drift free
of its focus on emerald green eyes. He shouted
out, "I see your head, I see your teeth, I see your
folded wings, and I see the hole in your belly below;
all encased in the wall of stone in front of me."
"That's better, boy. Now put down that hammer,
sit and let me speak," said the voice of Gregore
the Great. "Dragon's tarnished reputations as beasts
are blasphemy, distorted and quite undeserved.
We flew because we had wings to fly.
We spit flames from the fire pots that burned
deep within our tormented bellies.
We are winged creatures of prey that killed
to eat and live, just like you and all other things
living, born on land or the waters of the planet
humans named earth; the blue-green speck
lost within the Milky Way, itself a mere dot
of faint, fleeting light in our grand universe.
It's the same planet that I, Gregore the Great,
named Avian, in honor of the winged creatures
I adored; a species I sought to protect,
to keep unharmed, if only they would,
as loyal subjects, faithfully follow
a small list of rules I proclaimed as law.
The boy nodded, then said, "I seem to have heard
this story before, or at least one very similar
to what you have said. But what about my
grandfather, the injured man asleep in a coma,
who I fear is dying on his hospital bed?"
"I meant him no harm. His intrusion, your
unauthorized excursion, startled me from ten-thousand
years of a negligent sleep as I crept closer to death.

In a reflex response, I blew the poor old man aside,
but I swear I never intended to create a riptide."
Tears rolled down the checks of the boy
from the water that had welled in his eyes.
"I have to leave to collect the cam hooks
we used to climb down to the ledge
beside your place in this wall of stone,
and get home. My dad will be back
to take my mom, and my sister and I, later
today, to see grandpa before the doctors
unhook some tubes that are bothering him."
"Don't leave yet, boy," Gregore implored.
"I'm sorry the old man was hurt. I'm sorry
for the thousands and thousands of hurts
that I might have caused on this earth.
If you are brave, little boy, and trust
I mean good, I believe you can help save
the old man and free me as well from
the curse of the too-long near dead."
"You can make my grandfather well,"
asked the boy. Gregore answered, "No,
I said you would be the one who could help
the old man and me be free of our maladies."
Our son told my wife and I long afterwards
that he said to the dragon, "Gregore the Great,
I am ready for whatever it takes to bring back
my grandfather from his frightening sleep."
"Boy, listen closely," Gregore said, "my body
has hardened and molded itself in what was once
a large cave. The only entrance that remains
is the hole in my belly that burst from inside,
ripping apart the armor plates protecting me
from the harm that loomed outside of what I
thought was my impenetrable, warrior frame.
Inside that hole in my belly, near the back
of the cave you will find a small, smooth black rock

that is no longer too hot to hold, and is too still
for human hands to feel the faint pulse of life
beating within what to a human's eye
is no more than an ordinary rock or stone."
The boy crawled on his stomach to enter
the cave through the dragon's ruptured belly.
"I'm inside, but there are hundreds of rocks
lying around. I don't have time to sift and search
when they are all the same shape, color, and size."
"Turn out that damned light boy," the frustrated
dragon replied. "Close your eyes for a minute,
breathe deep, let go of the thoughts troubling
your mind. Now open your eyes and look
in the dark for the stone with the faint glow.
There is only one that remains with the primal
heat that sustains the life left within my mortally
wounded, stone-hardened shell."
"I see it, Gregore," the excited boy shouted.
"Now, what do I do with it?" he asked.
The dragon sighed with relief and said,
"Pick it up carefully with your hands, place
it safe in a pocket in your pants, then come
out of the hole in my belly to the light
outside, by the rock you call Indian Ledge.
"You're correct, it's warm, not hot, in my pocket
right here," said the boy as he proudly pointed
to the front pants pocket on his right side.
"Now gather your evidence as you leave,
and be quick as the polished stone will not
stay warm long after it is taken from me.
Get to wherever your grandfather sleeps
and place the stone in the palm of his left
hand. Close his fingers and grasp his fist
in your right hand. Hold it tight for however
long it takes your closed eyes to see a red glow."
"Thank you, Gregore, King of Avian, friend

of mine," said the boy to the dragon that he
had misunderstood. "I'll be back again
as soon as my grandfather no longer sleeps."
"I won't be here," Gregore replied. "When
you leave my green emerald eyes will close,
and when the stone glows red and the old man
wakes up I will at last be free, nothing more
of substance than a large fossilized stone."
"That's not fair," shouted the roused little boy.
"Little one, some say that life itself is not fair
with the circumstances and time that it parcels out.
You will eventually decide for yourself if that rings
true or not to the core of your soul. But for me,
Gregore the Great, once a King of Avian,
I am at a place of peace too long delayed.
I will know a rest that has no end. I can say
to my species, 'It is done, I am released.'
I know that one kind act does not erase
ten-thousand wrongs, but I am grateful
to do the right thing even if my soul's
everlasting redemption is not obtained.
Now, quick, finish your secret mission;
the polished stone must have a new home.
I promise you; I'll live on in your dreams.
Don't be afraid to tell your mother, sister,
father, and grandfather of our talk in my cave.
I'm sure, friend boy, as a man you will
have stories to tell, many more than just one
of a lonely, misguided dragon such as me."

Photos

Circa 1907 Photo: Alexander (seated), Mollie, James, and Allen McCollum

Ira and Hannah Kyle-McCollum Monument

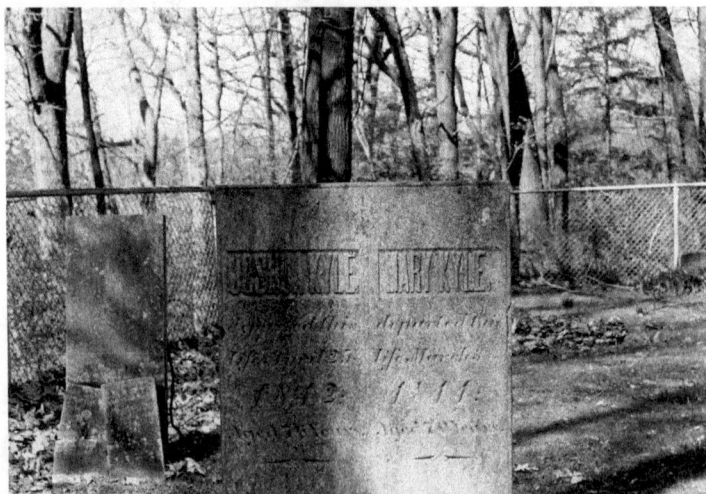

Joshua and Mary Stewart-Kyle Marker

Kyle-McCollum Historic Homestead

Old Home Cemetery

Idora's Ballroom

Idora's Empty Carousel

Idora's Empty Pool

Idora's Empty Sarcophagus

Idora Park, Enter at Own Risk

Idora's French Fry Stand

Idora's Ghost Coaster

Idora's Wildcat

Beware of Trolls

Lanterman's Falls

Stone Bridge

Suspension Bridge

The Wantanabi